THE ELASTIC BAND

Adventures In Christian Youth Ministry Through Music

Ros Oswald

First published in Great Britain

All paper used in the printing of this book has been made from wood grown in managed, sustainable forests.

ISBN13: 978-1-78003-672-4

Printed and bound in the UK
Pen Press is an imprint of
Indepenpress Publishing Limited
25 Eastern Place
Brighton
BN2 1GJ

A catalogue record of this book is available from the British Library

Cover design by Chris Oswald

UP & RUNNING MINISTRY

The Elastic Band

Introduction

I was born in 1954 and so I was a teenager in the 1960's when pop and rock music burst onto the scene. My biggest ambition was to play keyboard in a rock band. I was female, serious minded, and had strict parents. In other words, it was never going to happen. However, by listening to God (however reluctantly) my dream came true in spectacular fashion at 4 am on the main stage in Salisbury Cathedral at the All Night Youth Festival in July 1996.

This book explains how that happened. It also gives practical help and advice on how to develop your youth work in a way that really connects with young people. I started the Band in 1993, as a follow on to a mission at our local comprehensive school run by British Youth For Christ. I had no youth work training or formal music qualifications. I am certain that I could have done many things better and there are plenty of things I should not have done. However, over 15 years later the Band is remembered and talked about by parents, members of the congregation and old Band members. I hope this book will enable you to share in the fun and excitement that we enjoyed. I also hope it will encourage you to try out your own experiment for the benefit of your young people. Who knows – you might even find your own dream is realised.

Rosalind Oswald

March 2013

CONTENTS

HOW TO USE THIS BOOK

The purpose of this book is to enable and inspire you to set up your own Elastic Band, so you need to know what one is. An Elastic Band is a Band for young people (aged about 11 to 18) which has no auditions, is ecumenical and is not a worship group although it will play in worship situations. It is intended as a vehicle to enable you to get to know your young people better and to have fun being with them.

It does not work if it is set up to convert them, or to provide you with music in church because you are stuck for some musicians.

The focus of the Band has to be the well being of the young people and you have to enjoy just being with them if the Band is to thrive. You do not have to be a great musician (they will be far better than you eventually as they have more time to practice) but you do have to be willing to put in hours of preparatory work to keep everything ticking over (we will give you guidance about this throughout the book).

When I started the Band I was 39 years old and working full time. I had two children aged 8 and 5 and was not exactly looking for more work. On the music side I was a grade 6 pianist and had an O level in music. I could get a tune out of a recorder and a violin but I had no formal music teaching skills. Susie was younger than me, had one child and was working part time. We both lived in the village of Aldbourne which has a population of 1782 and worshipped at the Anglican church in the village. The village also has a Methodist church and we were quite happy to worship there as well. The two churches had a fairly good working relationship although joint services which had taken place every month at one time had come to an end. Joint services at Festival times such as Easter and Christmas were and are still held. The village is in Wiltshire and is in the Salisbury Diocese. We both taught in the Sunday School. So far as music training is concerned Susie did not have any but very much enjoyed lively worship and dance.

The Band started because there had been a mission at the local Comprehensive School in Marlborough by British Youth For Christ and a surprising number of young people from Aldbourne had taken a keen interest in this. As a result Just Looking groups were set up in the village. At the end of the Just Looking course (which was about eight weeks long) the interest remained.

We thought about how we could keep the impetus going – various suggestions were having a drama group, having a Bible study group, and my contribution was to suggest having a Band, if young people were interested. The other ideas did not seem to last long but the idea of the Band seemed to catch young people's imagination and enthusiasm. The young people who decided to become involved got a great deal out of it and in addition to that I felt that this was something worthwhile. It made sense for me at that stage in my spiritual journey but looking back I am astounded at the way that events unfolded. I was able to fulfill many secret ambitions that I had had since my own childhood. Wherever the Band seemed ready to go, doors simply opened. It's my experience that whenever you follow God's will for your life, He'll take you to places you could hardly dream of.

In the past I had never enjoyed playing with other musicians unless they had some idea of how to play.

When I was praying about the idea of starting the Band I distinctly remember saying in the prayer

"God, I am prepared to run this Band but please don't put me in a room with a few out of tune recorders."

Nineteen years on, I can think of nothing I would rather do and within a very short space of time the recorders can be producing music that any congregation would be happy to hear – yes honestly that is what happened.

From the start I kept a careful written record of what we did, what happened at the Band meetings and what we played. This has proved invaluable as time has gone by and I hope it will help you in deciding if this type of work is for you. Throughout the book you will find examples of the newsletters that we distributed and the yearly reports we produced. I have done this not because I feel they are particularly good examples of what to do but to show you how we changed and developed as time went by. Also, you can see that we were just ordinary people doing our best to relate to our young people.

We always felt that the point of the Band was to hang out together whilst playing music. How the week had gone at school and at home was always as important if not more so than the music we were playing. On one occasion when there was an important international football match on the boys rehearsed wearing their Walkmans and a cheer went up every time a goal was scored. We were trying to practice for an important Festival at the time but we preferred the boys to come and want to be with us rather than drop out and watch the match at home as I am sure they would have preferred.

On another very poignant occasion a boy in our village (not a Band member) had died tragically and suddenly. He had been buried that week in the graveyard behind the church where we practiced. Again, we were preparing for an important event but that night we talked about how we felt about what had happened. As a collective act we gathered around the grave and sang a quiet worship song in his memory. This was a very special moment for all the Band. In the Diary Section I will describe this in more detail.

In part one of this book (the Diary) I will take you through the development of the Band explaining what happened, and why. In part two I will then give you pointers towards setting up your own Band. Please remember that it must be your Band. It will not be right to do exactly what we did even if you wanted to. Every place and every child is different and must be respected as the individuals they are. However, when we started it would have been great to have a few ideas to draw on and some suggestions of things to avoid!

I read as many books about youth work as I could lay my hands on. Some were very useful but none of them touched on the idea of running a Band in any detail. They also seemed designed for much larger churches with more resources. At the start we had no money, no books and just a room to rehearse and meet in. That was it. By the ending of the Band we had earned fees for playing at Festivals and we donated our travel expenses to the band. We had enough money to buy some flags and percussion instruments for our churches in Aldbourne to use in the future. They are still in use now. We also had enough left to invest £100 in a fair trade organisation named Shared Interest who had sent a speaker to a service at which we had played.

An important principle for Susie and I from the beginning was that there would be no limit to the size of the Band and no rules about attendance. We tried to have as few rules as possible as we wanted the kids to want to be there and having to monitor their attendance did not fit in with our ideas. The point about the name of the Band was that the Band had to be Elastic enough to welcome everyone. One of the few rules we did have was that we would play at least some Christian music at every practice and any non-Christian songs we used (such as "Everything I Do" from Robin Hood Prince of Thieves or "Tears in Heaven" by Eric Clapton) had to be at least consistent with Christian principles. If a band member wanted me to listen to some satanic death metal music because they were interested in it, then I would do that outside rehearsal time so that we could talk about it. However, the rehearsal time would not be taken up with it. This seemed to work well and we were able to discuss the music scene generally whilst playing a great deal of worship music over the years.

So lets lift the veil on the Elastic Band and take you with us on our journey. If you have already decided that running a Band is for you feel free to ignore the Diary and go straight for the "How To" sections. Or, even better, just start the Band!

Part 1:

Diary

Year One
1993

GET SERIOUS, JOSHUA, IT'LL NEVER WORK.

The first nine months

I moved to the village of Aldbourne in Wiltshire (population 1782) in 1985 with my husband Chris and our daughter Elly who was born earlier that year. I started worshipping at the Anglican village church of St. Michaels. The village also had and still has a Methodist church. Our vicar lived in the village. I helped out in the Sunday School as I had always enjoyed working with children. I was a competent but very amateur musician (grade 6 piano). In 1988 our second child Nikki was born. I was working part time from 1985 onwards but had to work full time from 1992

It was during the winter of 1992/3 that British Youth For Christ (BYFC) ran a mission at the Comprehensive school in Marlborough. We had been advised in advance by BYFC to have in place "Just Looking" groups for the benefit of any young people who responded positively to the mission. We were very surprised at the number of people from Aldbourne who did respond (given the small size of the village) but we were able to provide groups for all of them. I assisted in the running of one group. The course lasted for eight weeks. It was during those weeks that I began to feel that it was right for me to offer to run a Band if the young people were interested.

I went to Spring Harvest for the second time in the Spring of 1993 and spoke to as many people as possible to get some help and advice. I went to every seminar I could find on either worship or youth work. I was unable to find anyone who had done exactly what I was planning to do. However, I did gain some helpful support and advice from the seminars. The main messages I took away were these:

Don't pretend to be young yourself.
Even worse, don't try to be cool and/or trendy. It's just fake and will be spotted a mile away by any young person.

Have a realistic and measurable aim that you can check yourself as you go on.
Get on with it.

The first piece of advice took a lot of the pressure away. Feeling a real passion for the young people and their spiritual development was more important than being able to recite the words (if any) of the songs in the top 20 or knowing all of the England football players.

With regard to an aim, I decided that this was to introduce as many young people as possible to good, relevant Christian music. Nineteen years later I know that this aim was fulfilled. If things were going badly when the Band was running (as they sometimes did), I could always go back to this aim and it helped me to retain my focus. In some ways we exceeded the aim or at least we went beyond the simple interpretation of it. Band members wrote songs themselves, led worship, set up their own Band, played for children's and youth festivals and raised money for Children in Need. However, by retaining that one simple aim, it was always possible to make sure that the Band did not turn into a secular youth group or become too introspective.

The advice to get on with it came from John Ritter who, with his wife Sue, was running the 12 – 14 year groups at Spring Harvest that year. He was supportive and said that the best way to do this was to get together a group of like-minded people and then make a start........ Here is the first Elastic Band Factsheet ....

Bring your favourite instrument

When? Tuesdays 6.30 - 7.30

Where? Methodist Hall

First Session - 18th May 1993

Music:

1.	All of my heart	(Kids Praise 1)
2.	Brand New Song	(Kids Praise 2)
3.	There's nobody else like Jesus	(Kids Praise 14)
4.	I believe in Jesus	(Mission Praise 264, or Spring Harvest '91 43 or Spring Harvest '93 49)

For problems, queries or a chat ring:

Ros Oswald - 40619 or
Catherine Coates - 40578 or
Sue May - 40642

With more enthusiasm than experience we held our first Elastic Band meeting. We had asked the young people who had attended the Just Looking groups if they would be interested in joining a Band. The response had been sufficiently positive to encourage us to go ahead. At this time the "us" consisted of me and my friends Susie May and Catherine Coates. After a couple of sessions it was clear that Catherine was more comfortable being a supporter than working face to face with the young people. However, Susie and I went on and worked together with the Band for five years until she moved to Lincolnshire.

Susie was a good enabler and because her skills were in communication and movement rather than music she helped to

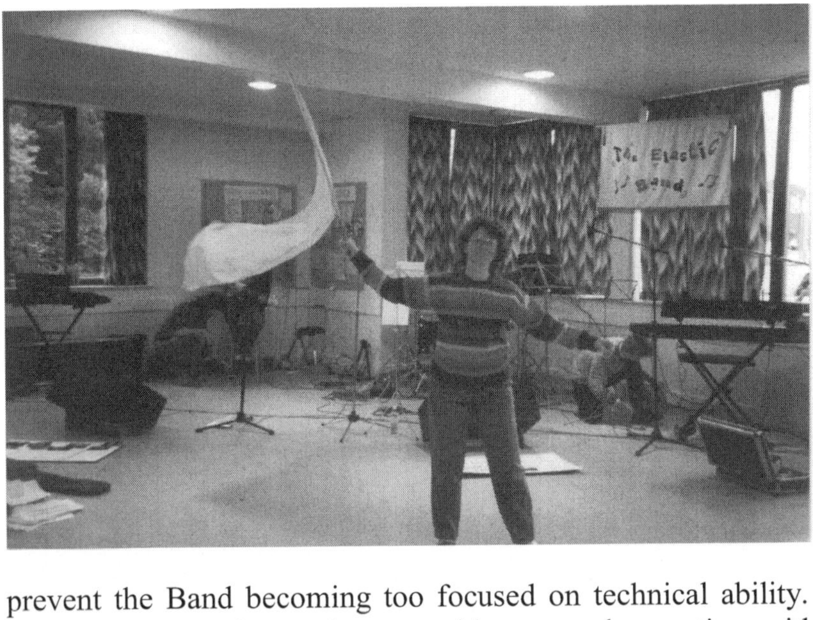

prevent the Band becoming too focused on technical ability. She worked part time and so was able to spend more time with the young people outside Band sessions than I was. She was also willing to spend time on the Band and to develop her skills.

So far as the first session was concerned, we had been given permission to use the Methodist Church Hall in the village free of charge. This was useful as we did not have any funds. We had designed a Newsletter and decided what songs to attempt.

We had no intention at that stage of ever playing in public and so did not have a deadline to meet which was very useful. We played games and quizzes as well as music so that we could enjoy just getting to know each other.

When we began, the regulations governing children work were less strict (this was 1993) but we kept notes of each session which were invaluable when we wanted to reflect on what we had done or were doing. Now, a register and detailed records would be a requirement together with parental consent forms.

Week One - 25th May 1993

Five enthusiastic boys attended the first session and the instruments were Clarinet, Eb Tenor Horn, Cornet and Violin. This was not the easiest set of instruments to combine especially bearing in mind the fact that three of them were transposing instruments (This means that music had to be written in a different key because the instrument by way of its construction transposes the key of the music) and violins can be tricky to tune. We encouraged the boys to design their own version of "Amen" and we played two songs I had learnt at Spring Harvest. Sue read out the prayer from the Bible Study Daily Notes she was using at the time. As this was a prayer for more organists, choristers and musicians, we felt this was a good start. Susie and I were feeling our way at this stage and quickly realized that it works well if you have plenty of different activities lined up, to keep the young people engaged. However the focus of the action was and remained the playing of Christian songs. The session lasted an hour which felt about right.

The boys were happy to come back the following week with their new versions of "Amen". I had taken some of my music stands and music and Susie had brought her tape recorder so that we would know what we sounded like. Fourteen years later, when I listen to the tapes I am surprised we kept going but the musical quality did improve considerably!

I made notes of each session from the beginning and used this to keep my register. They record that the boys were keen to talk about Guns N' Roses (a very popular band at the time). I was happy to do that because it enabled us to build up trust and lines of communication. However, I was aware that some of that band's lyrics were decidedly non-Christian. I agreed to listen to Guns N' Roses songs so we could talk about them but only outside the time set aside for our meeting. I was expecting to be asked to listen to some fairly extreme lyrics to see what my reaction would be. This is what happened but once I had made it clear that I would discuss the lyrics but only by having a calm and reasoned conversation, the initial interest died down.

Week two

We had seven attenders again but only two who were the same as from week one. The range of instruments was different as well, with recorders, flute and percussion. The Elastic Band was living up to its name and Sue and I had to be able to respond to whatever line up we were presented with. I had written a quiz based on Psalm 150 to establish how many instruments are referred to in the Psalm. I wanted to expand the knowledge about the use of music in church as much as possible. I knew we might encounter some resistance if we took different instruments into church services and I wanted the children to have confidence in what we were doing . I felt that by making sure they understood the Biblical background this would help.

We talked about the different things we could enjoy doing and meeting other musicians who could help improve our skills was a popular choice. I agreed to see what could be organized. We played two songs including a repeat of one from the week before and listened to the different settings for "Amen" The most memorable one for me was based on the Tarzan call from the films. I doubted whether it would be popular at a Matins Service but at least some effort had gone into working it out.

We had prepared another newsletter but as these were being used as paper aeroplanes we decided to start relying on verbal communication. Prayers were said at the start and end of each session by the leaders. However, we made it clear that we wanted everyone to be involved in the praying during the meetings and by the third session the Band members were saying their own prayers.

Co-incidentally, the Psalm which I had used to write the quiz was sung in church the following Sunday in the main service. This gave us great encouragement.

Week Three

We had 12 young people. Although it was early days we were starting to get a feel for how the sessions might work. They were lively and noisy but the young people were willing to say short prayers. We started to think about a logo for the Band. Eventually, the Elastic Band Man (You can see him on the cover of this book) became a recognizable part of our image.

From then on...

We had 13 sessions between our first one in May and the end of the summer holidays in August. It was very clear that there were enough young people wanting to come to make it a worthwhile exercise. During those first four months we carried out the following activities:

- We played Christian songs such as "Amazing Love", "Be Bold, Be Strong" , "Lord of Lords", "Majesty" and "Hosanna"
- We practiced improvising
- We completed the "Amen" competition having taped all the entries and a member of our congregation came to one

session and judged the entries (he was not related to any Band member)

- We listened to tapes of Christian bands such as Halo and Stryper and talked about them
- We played games such as gargling using lemonade and trying to guess the songs we were gargling
- I talked to the Methodist Minister about what we were doing and why. He listened to a tape of our playing and was encouraging. This was very important to Sue and me as leaders
- We asked the young people to complete a questionnaire so that we could see which directions they wanted to go in.

By the end of August we had had 16 different young people attending at least one session. Three who had attended the first session were still members when we drew the Band to a close five and a half years later.

We had tried to find the right balance between playing music, talking, playing games and talking about the Bible and praying. We were very fortunate that all the young people had been to at least some of the Youth for Christ mission at their school and most had been to a "Just Looking" group. It meant that we had a common starting point. In addition, the majority of the parents were sympathetic to and supportive of our aims. Some of them were actively involved in our village churches. This meant that we had invaluable backing from them. Without them we could not have achieved what we did.

We had to make a decision about what to do with the Band during the school holidays. We did not want to stop having Band sessions for a variety of reasons:

- We enjoyed ourselves
- We were all still keen to come
- It set us apart from school

- God does not go on holiday and we wanted to mirror, in some small way, the welcoming heart of God. I realize that does sound pretentious and over-ambitious but it was a genuine desire on the parts of Sue and me

However, holidays brought difficulties because attendance was patchy and so it was harder to plan. It did mean that we were able to try different ideas. I tried bringing a microphone and practice amplifier (this is a small amplifier suitable for home use). This proved extremely popular and I had to make sure access to it was fairly shared between those who wanted or needed to use it. It tended to be monopolized by one or two Band members. A number of the members had been to Christian Camps (such as Scripture Union) and brought new songs with them.

Another idea which worked well in the holidays was organising small groups to visit local musicians in their own homes. I was also busy making contacts with our Diocesan Youth Advisor. Support is tremendously important particularly with a new idea involving young people. I often felt that I would have welcomed a teacher or guide. I read as widely as possible, particularly on subjects relating to worship music and attitudes to children and young people. I did not find anything directly relevant but there was plenty of material emphasizing that my own lifestyle was as important as any amount of talking. This could be very challenging at times!

September

The most exciting news for the Band was that there were to be ecumenical informal youth services from September in our village and the Band was to provide the music. By now, it was the beginning of September, everyone was back from holiday and we were in full swing again. The prospect of playing for the services was met with great enthusiasm. We found that playing choruses such as "Hosannah" and "Majesty" from Mission Praise worked well. My husband, a keen if fairly inexperienced guitarist, had written some simplified accompaniments and I had written some simple parts for the other solo instruments. We found that the best approach was to play simple pieces well. Overambitious attempts at more complex pieces did not sound pleasant.

I had real reservations about playing in public because I wasn't sure what the music would sound like. We were still very raw and although some songs came together miraculously well, others didn't.

However, the Band members were very keen and I knew the congregation would be small and sympathetic – so it would never be any easier!

The first Ecumenical Youth Service was on the 12th September 1993 and there were ten Band members plus Sue and me. My diary written at the time says that it was "wonderful and amazing". I can be prone to exaggeration but at least it all happened. I had been in Chester playing keyboard for the Lawyers Christian Fellowship Conference and arrived back just in time to organize the setting up for the service. One of the parents said that my keyboard was too loud. Partly this was because after the dash from Chester I hadn't had time for a proper sound check. In addition, I think that I probably wanted to cover over anything that sounded a bit grim! I became more confident as we progressed. Here is the play list to give an indication of what worked for us:

PLAYLIST FOR BAND INFORMAL SERVICE ON THE 12TH SEPTEMBER 1993

During the service

1. Hosanna Mission Praise 242
2. Lord of Lords Mission Praise 883
3. Majesty Mission Praise 454

For the prayer time

4. Be Still 50
5. I'm Special 325

For the conclusion of the Service

6. I Give you Now Songs of Fellowship 211
7. Reconciled Mission Praise 568

NB The number for Lord of Lords is from a more recent edition of Mission Praise. We were using a Spring Harvest book at the time but it may be easier for you to locate in Mission Praise if you want to see what we actually played in our very early days.

The answers to the questionnaire Susie and I had prepared told us that we were playing music that most of the Band liked and most of the Band members were prepared to try harder songs. They all wanted to play for services and playing music themselves was what they wanted to do. Singing was less popular and praying was not popular at all. We clearly had more work to do to develop their spirituality. However, I was very pleased we had survived the first term and the young people had returned after the summer break.

By the 25th September I had handed over the role of keyboard player to one of our Band members which made my life easier. I also discussed some theory of worship with him. 19 years later he is still a good friend despite the age difference.

A week later we had eleven Band members and the session went well. Five days later we played for our second service with 13 Band members and according to my notes it was a "good experience of meeting with God". We had come a long way.

At the following Band session we played every song we knew! I realized that we needed a capo for the guitars. This is a device which shortens the strings and makes the fingering easier on some pieces. I was having to develop my musical knowledge as we went along – especially how to write simple parts for transposing instruments and a very wide range of musical ability. I was determined that no-one should be excluded because of a lack of skill.

I was also reading up about the history of church music. I had found out about the village bands that were in common use before the organ became so prevalent. I was able to find some drawings to show the Band members. One of these showed a Church Gallery Band from 1835 with a bassoon, flute, viol and clarinet. Perhaps we weren't breaking as much new ground as I had thought!

As we became the resident band for the informal Sunday evening services the rehearsals acquired a greater focus which the young people enjoyed. Our profile was also being raised as we were referred to and prayed for in one of the Anglican church services.

October

Finding a place to rehearse was a problem which existed (to some extent) throughout the life of the Band. We had no funds and so had to rely on one or other of the churches (Anglican or Methodist) to offer us a home. The Anglican church hall needed extensive repairs and (as we discovered on the 19th October 1993) the table tennis club were a regular fee paying booking for the Methodist Hall. As a result we were evicted but were able to use the Methodist church building.

The third service came around very quickly. It was half term, which always affected the numbers but there were still eight members present plus Sue and me. The time just before the service was always difficult as plenty of help was needed with stands, music and tuning instruments. We had no money to buy books and so that was a real problem. There is more about what to do about this in Part 2 Section 2.5 paragraph 7. I spent many not very happy hours crawling about on our lounge floor trying to put together sheets of music and unscrambling the mess left behind after the last rehearsal or service. Don't let the young people take music home with them – it will be either lost or forgotten.

By now we were getting to know the band members better and settling in to the idea of playing for the Informal Services.

I suggested that we write reviews for other church members of contemporary Christian Bands and lent out some of my tapes and CDs for this purpose. I didn't see a single review but my one to one conversations with different band members convinced me that they did listen to at least some of the tracks.

November

As we were approaching Christmas, we planned a Christmas party and held a rap competition for all the Band members. The rap had to be based on a Christian theme. We played for a Christian Aid Service on the 11th November 1993 and an Informal Service on the 14th November.

The service on the 14th November was a memorable one as the congregation actually marched round the church to "I am the Way"! I realize that for some congregations that would be normal. In our rural Church of England parish it was not. Throughout the life of the Band I felt that we gave the adult congregation (with a few exceptions) permission to be more relaxed in worship and to be open to new ways to express themselves. I valued their openness and tried not to overdo the use of unfamiliar songs which can so easily alienate even the most sympathetic church member.

On the 20th November we organized a concert in the village by Keep in Step which is made up of two well known Christian artists Sue & John Ritter.

December

We held the rap competition on the 7th December and had six Band members taking part. The Christmas party was on the 14th at the home of two of our Band members whose parents were particularly supportive. We had a visit from a Christian drummer on the 22nd December. He had brought a great deal of kit with him and was happy to let the Band members experiment. His visit was extremely popular. There were 13 Band members there.

At this point we paused to draw breath over Christmas. It had been an exhausting nine months but we now had a core of regular attenders and a play list to work from. We were stronger on relationships with Band members than musical ability but there were some improvements that had taken place. Both Sue and I felt we had come a long way.

I used the Christmas break to write a review about the Band's activities. It was a useful exercise and I did this each year the Band was functioning.

Year Two

1994

January to May

We were off to a great start having been asked to provide the worship for an all day event organized by British Youth for Christ in our local town. One of the band members had a broken wrist but was able to provide percussion instead of his usual clarinet. It was the first time we had played for anyone other than our local congregation .The day went well and when the young people attending were asked how they might want to progress their faith one of them suggested starting an Elastic Band in their church. This felt very encouraging.

Sue and I spent time praying about our vision for the Band and also had positive feed back from our village Ecumenical Committee and at our local church AGM. We had prepared a display of photos and information about the Band. Humour was always in evidence when we were around and I noticed a prayer request for "the surefootedness of Morris dancers". This support was absolutely essential as we were putting in a great deal of time and effort. Without practical and spiritual support we would have run out of energy very quickly.

April

We continued playing for our village informal services and met on a weekly basis. The drum kit appeared with a very enthusiastic but inexperienced drummer. Some 14 years later he was in a group of us that went to Spring Harvest and we were able to share lots of good memories about the Band. It was a real joy to see him and his faith develop through his teenage years.

We sent out another questionnaire to the Band members here is my analysis of the results.

Question 1 If the Elastic Band was an animal what would it be

Answers Snail, slug, cow, unicorn, eagle, sabre tooth tiger, lion.

Question 2 From now on what would you like the Elastic band to do

Answers Guns 'n Roses, Metallica, Ice T have fun, worship the Lord, play the gargling game, dance to the music, play music and play games

Question 3 Have you played with the Elastic band at any informal services the BYFC fired up event, the Christian Aid evening

Answers - Yes = 8

Question 4 How did you feel about it and would you like to play again in that situation

Answers I enjoyed playing even though I played some wrong chords - It was very fun to do - Inspired - I enjoyed this very much especially shutting the mans car in

Question 5 Do you feel being involved with the band has increased your knowledge of Jesus

Answers Yes = 7 sort of = 1

Question 6 Do you feel being involved with the band has improved your playing

Answers Yes = 7 No = 1

Question 7 Do you feel being involved with the band has improved your gargling

Answers Yes = 6 No = 2

Question 8 Is there anything else you would like the band to do that we havent done yet

Answers

Guns 'n Roses, Metallica, Alice in Chains, Learn some new songs, play at Wembley Stadium, review Christian music, go to Christian gigs play at the Royal Albert Hall

Question 9 What other musicians would you like to meet

Answers

Drummers guitarists Chris Rea Axl Rose Roger Waters Paul McCartney Mouth organist didgeridooist

It was at this point that my husband started to help with the running of the Band. At first it was behind the scenes. He put all my music into folders so we could find it more easily. I also had help from our local music shop as I asked them to help me understand more about drums. I was very pleasantly surprised to find a real desire to help a Christian band when the shop decorations tended towards heavy metal.

May

We had a competition for Band members based on Psalm 149 verse 3. It was becoming clear that some of the boys struggled with the dancing and action songs we did but when it came to playing for workshops or informal services they took their playing seriously. By the 31st May 1994 we had been going for a full 12 months and my diary entry contains one word

"Hallelujah!"

The weekly Band sessions continued and, wherever possible we tried to weave Bible knowledge into our singing and playing. One of the Band's favourite songs was "Blessed is the King who comes in the Name of the Lord". We asked the Band to tell us where to find the reference to this in the Bible. They got there with some help and from then on we tried to include memory verses in our repertoire from time to time.

June

We wrote to a number of well-known bands including Alice in Chains and Guns N' Roses. Each letter was signed by all the members of the Band. We wrote to seven in all and received replies from two of them. Both bands who replied were run by Christians – this point was not overlooked by the band members.

Sue and I were very aware of our complete lack of training for the work we were doing and asked if we could attend a course in Salisbury. It lasted over a weekend and looked at creativity in worship. We were funded by the PCC (the course cost £30) and we gained a lot from talking to others. No one was doing what we were trying to do but those we spoke to were very supportive.

July and August

By now we were gaining in confidence musically and we planned the songs to play as a group. Our times of open prayer were becoming less stilted. We still kept them short and the prayers might include praying for someone who was ill or praying for a new bass guitar for a Band member.

We had nine Band members playing on the 10th July 1994 at an informal service which also included dance and drama. An adult member of the congregation asked for the words to "I'm Special". She had not heard it before and it had clearly touched her.

We also had another visit from a local adult professional musician, a friend of Sue's. He talked about playing guitars, played some music himself and helped our young guitarists. It was a popular session.

One of the Band members brought a French exchange student to a rehearsal. I did wonder what on earth he thought of us!

We were still holding competitions on various themes and our local Methodist Minister called in to judge the competition for setting Psalm 149 verse 3 to a new tune. He was always very supportive of us and when he moved to a different church about 20 miles away, invited us to play there.

We started planning for a Harvest Festival service. One Band member chose the music, another worked out a dance using ribbons and a third wrote a song. Sue and I had seen the ribbons used at Spring Harvest. Although we weren't very expert, they added colour.

Another local Christian musician (this time a drummer) came along to help our young drummer who, unfortunately, about this time had a serious car accident (prayer needed!) He was brought to a service 12 days after his accident in which he broke his leg and collarbone and he returned to rehearsals two weeks later still with a plaster cast on his leg!

We had a change of venue to the Old Craft Room. The building belonged to the Church and was in serious need of repair. As a result, bits of plaster tended to fall on our heads if the drummer got too enthusiastic.

September

By this stage there were some differences appearing between the boys who wanted an electric guitar approach and the girls who enjoyed dance and using ribbons. This was an ongoing problem and two of the girls decided to leave the Band as a result. I was very saddened by this but felt I had to respect their decision, as did Sue.

At the time, we did not know where the Band would take us and this could feel isolating. I found this period around September 1994 to January 1995 a very difficult one. It was as if we were on a roller coaster in the dark. All we could do was press on and pray that we were within God's purposes for the Band.

By now, we were playing regularly for informal services and the emphasis had shifted from an internal to an external perspective. The songs we were using included I will build my church, I want to worship the Lord, Shine Jesus Shine, Spirit of the Living God. The bass guitar which had been prayed for duly arrived. We would usually have 9 or 10 young people at each practice and service.

The other local villages were expressing a desire to have a similar youth band of their own. This resolved by having young people from surrounding villages join our band. Sue and I were conscious that the relationships in the Band were crucial to how the Band functioned. As I wrote in my diary on the 27th September "Sue thought we should turn the Band into a dating agency – perhaps it already is!"

We had been asked to play for an informal service even though I was away. I had my reservations but knew how important it was for the Band to be able to function whether I was there or not. With some serious practicing and lots of prayer, the service went well which was a real confidence boost for our young people. The unstated aim which Sue and I had was that one day, the young people would form their own Christian Band and we would be redundant. Read on to see what actually happened!

October

We used the half term practice to plan the next service. We had two band members there as the others were away. It was very encouraging to see how seriously they took the task. We used the songs "I will build my church" and "The church is not a building" regularly. I like to think that repeatedly singing those words helped both us and the congregation to think about these important issues more deeply.

November

This month had its ups and downs. A very kind and talented member of the congregation made a banner for us and we made a start on interactive worship where we invited the congregation to write parts for a song. Here is an example of one song we wrote for this purpose. It has worked very well in a lot of different settings and always results in a heated debate (usually about the football!).

JEW OR GENTILE

Here are the words of a song which has been designed to be re written for every congregation that sings it! You will see that there are blank spaces which we will be filling in during the service. We hope you enjoy the song and the song writing.

CHORUS
Jew or gentile slave or free
If you come from Galilee
…………..or Aldbourne too
Work together see what God can do

VERSE ONE
I like watching ………on TV
You like watching …………
One Corinthians says we must agree
And put our differences behind us

CHORUS
Jew or gentile slave or free
If you come from Galilee
…………..or Aldbourne too
Work together see what God can do

VERSE TWO
……………………..are the best
I like watching…………………
One Corinthians says we must agree
And put our differences behind us

CHORUS
Jew or gentile slave or free
If you come from Galilee
…………..or Aldbourne too
Work together see what God can do

VERSE THREE
I like..............you think they're the pits
You like ....
One Corinthians says we must agree
And put our differences behind us

CHORUS
Jew or gentile slave or free
If you come from Galilee
.............or Aldbourne too
Work together see what God can do

To give you some clues the first verse is about television programmes, the second verse is about football teams and the third verse is about styles of music. So start thinking about all your favourites and lets see if they will fit in! Remember though what One Corinthians has to say!

We also provided worship at a Churches Together event in a local village. I was very proud of the way the band members contributed.

We also played for an informal service in our own church and included the song "Be Bold, Be Strong" (a real Band favourite). Micky, our drummer, liked to emphasise the words "I am not afraid, No!, No!, No!" We were left in no doubt as to how he felt about being afraid – or rather not feeling afraid. The Band induced a confident feeling in the congregation by their enthusiasm. It is only with the benefit of hindsight that I can see how very valuable a gift that can be.

Despite there being very encouraging times, November was a difficult month. We lost two of our female members as they were not enjoying the music (their words). As the electric instruments had started arriving, the feel of the Band had changed and it was more suited to the boys we had. I felt very upset at our loss but decided to let the Band take its course. From the extensive reading I was doing about youth work I was aware that keeping teenage boys connected with Church was a very real issue. Therefore, I decided to stick with the electric route rather than try to stay acoustic. There is a section on this important issue in Part 2 of this book to help you make your own decisions.

November was also a time I started feeling very tired. We had been running the Band with a very short break since May the previous year and were spending about 10 hours per week on it. My diary note for the 29th November reads;

> "I'm losing energy when people don't practice, don't come when they say they will and don't listen. Help God!"

This really is exactly how it felt sometimes and it's good to know that this is normal and God will help you to keep going, provided you ask Him to.

December.

We were asked to play for the Carols by Candlelight service which is one of our village's most important Festival Services.

This helped to give us some focus and then it was the end of the year and time to prepare my Newsletter. I loved writing these because it enabled me to look back on what we had done and just how far we had come. It's very obvious that my very limited computer skills did develop as the years went by.

Year Three

1995

January

We had an enforced break as most of the Band were in the village Panto which was rehearsing on Mondays and Wednesdays. We started back on the 31st January and started planning what we would play for the service when the Bishop was due to come.

February

By now, the membership had settled down to a committed core of boys. They wanted to play guitars and use drums and they formed a very good basis both musically and in terms of fellowship. One of my notes for February reads;

> "It was really good just to have fun and talk together"

This, for me, was the main difference between a worship group and a Band. We did play worship music and when our rehearsals were going well I felt a real sense of the presence of the Holy Spirit coming in power. However, our focus was always on the spiritual development of our Band members and not on the music for the next service.

With the benefit of hindsight, the 12th February 1995 was a turning point for the Band because we played for the Sunday School. What we learned as time went by was that the Band excelled at providing excellent worship songs for groups of younger children. It was a very exciting and energizing mix and led to some amazing experiences as you will see. It gave the Band members confidence to be seen as musicians in their own right.

In February one of our members, Tim, came with an electric guitar. We were able to help him as he acquired a better technique and the arrival of the electrical equipment encouraged my husband Chris to join in more as well. Our daughter, Elly, who was 10 years old was also interested in joining. The boys were a few years older than her (and considerably noisier as she played the flute) but the mix of young people we had worked well.

March

We had been asked to provide a display about the Band for the PCC Annual General Meeting. We always spent some time in each session looking for good new songs to add to our playlist. We found that, provided the songs were good, the congregation were willing to join in and learn them.

Favourites at this time included "Lord I lift Your Name on High" (with an Elastic Band rock riff) and "Father God I wonder". We played for an informal service which went well and included a song about Jonah which I had written for the Band. We also welcomed back Russell who was and remains a very talented keyboard player. He was valuable to me in particular as his presence meant that I could focus on worship leading and making sure everyone else had a good idea of what they were doing or supposed to be doing. It was wonderful to see the young people becoming more and more skilled in their musicianship as well as more comfortable at playing for worship

April

We played for an informal service but had to use a backing tape as I wasn't around. Once Russell had got his confidence we didn't need to use backing tapes but this was early days for him. The tape wasn't very successful and reinforced the need for real live musicians. The tape was inflexible and the less able musicians were unable to play along with it.

We had been asked to play for the main 11.00 am service in the Anglican Church in the village. The Band members were all very excited at this opportunity as it was a big step up for them from the informal services. Mark, our bass player, brought the biggest amplifier with him that I had ever seen. Fortunately, we received positive feedback from the adult members of the congregation who had not heard the Band before. Bearing in mind that our weekly worship was accompanied only by an organ, this showed a very open-minded spirit on the part of the congregation.

May

Another big step forward for the Band. Two new female band members arrived from the next village, a flautist and a guitar player. This brought the male/female balance in the Band to 5 male and 6 female including myself, Sue and my husband Chris. We also welcomed another leader, Paul, who offered to look after the mixing desk for us. We needed to be amplified because of the nature of the instruments and the arrival of the drum kit.

This made life much more complicated in some ways (see Chapter 2.4 on the acoustic/non-acoustic debate) but it felt like the right way to go at the time. Also, in May, I asked the PCC for funding for four Mission Praise books for the Band. We had struggled a lot to work out how to have the music organized. Some of the guitarists preferred to play from words and chord symbols only, some used words and chord letters, some singers wanted just words. This is a difficult area and so Chapter 2.5 tells you how we coped. The PCC approved the funding which was a great help and encouragement for us.

We expanded our play list and the new members had some helpful suggestions. We distributed the play list to people organizing the services we played for. This helped to make sure that we weren't asked to play new pieces at very short notice. Here is the list that I used to hand out to let the service organizers know what was possible.

REPERTOIRE

1. Reconciled
2. Be Bold Be Strong
3. Easter Song
4. Moses Song
5. All of My Heart
6. I believe in Jesus
7. Only by Grace
8. Come on and Celebrate
9. Brand New Song
10. I believe in Jesus
11. Jesus
12. Jesus is Greater
13. Lets Praise God together
14. There's nobody like Jesus
15. Lord of Lords King of Kings
16. We Rejoice in the Grace of God
17. Brother let me be Your Servant
18. Glory
19. Majesty
20. Hosanna
21. We are Gathered
22. Lord you put a Tongue in my Mouth
23. You shall go out with Joy
24. Exalted
25. The Church is not a Building
26. God is on Fire.
27. Shine Jesus Shine
28. I will Build my Church
29. Blessed be the Name of the Lord
30. Holy Spirit we welcome you
31. I am a new Creation
32. Coming of the King

33. I was once in Darkness
34. When I survey the Wondrous Cross
35. What a friend we have in Jesus
36. I'm special
37. Jesus we celebrate
38. Rejoice
39. Prayer is like a telephone
40. The Battle belongs to the Lord
41. Jew or Gentile
42. I want to serve the Purpose of God
43. Spirit of the Living God
44. I want to worship the Lord
45. Stand up Stand up for Jesus
46. Amazing Love
47. Father God I wonder
48. You are Crowned
49. The Crucible for Silver
50. Blessed is the King who comes
51. God made Noses
52. Angels
53. We are here to praise you
54. One shall tell another
55. Tell out my soul
56. Go (I give you now)
57. Thine be the Glory
58. Lord I lift your name on high
59. Tell out Tell out good news
60. Everything I Do
61. Tears in Heaven
62. The Gift
63. Ho – ho – holy spirit
64. Brother let me be your servant
65. Only by Grace

There were some interesting snippets in my diary for May. My husband heard someone singing "Shine Jesus Shine" in the toilets when he was at College one evening. "Silver and Gold" was suggested as a new (to us) song for us to learn and it then cropped up in Sue's Bible Study notes for the week.

A mission had been planned for the village to take place in October. We were very keen to bring our unique blend of energy and humour to this important event. Sarah, one of our new Band members, suggested we try to break a world record, if we could think of one. We also played, in May, for an informal service. The newly purchased Mission Praise music books arrived and were very welcome. We also looked at the rules for the Guinness Book of Records and came up with the idea of writing a song based on verses from the Bible, performing it at a service of at least 25 people, publishing it and selling at least 25 copies in one afternoon! We had to write to the Guinness Book of Records for their official sanction.

There was also a confirmation service in May at which two of our Band members were due to play. They were worried about the music so we spent time helping them. Our books were borrowed by the church for that service but returned afterwards.

June

It was in June that we started putting together the music for a "Make Way" event. There are a series of these written by Graham Kendrick. They are intended as outreach events and the one I was particularly interested in was "Make Way for Christmas" or "The Gift". I haven't recorded why we decided to do it, but originally I bought it at Spring Harvest as an interesting booklet. However, we were becoming more ambitious for the Band now. I felt that the Band was able to inject our worship in the village with both physical and spiritual energy. I wanted as many people as possible to experience this.

Our sessions were enabling our members to talk about concerns they had. Tim was concerned that at a Metallica gig, 50,000 people had been making the sign of the Devil. At least we could pray about this. We also helped Tim work out how to use his newly acquired effects pedal.

Within one week of seeing the music for "The Gift", Russ, our keyboard player, had got his head round the music. We also spent time trying to find easier chords for some of the songs we would be playing at our next informal service. Neither Sue nor I were guitarists but by talking as a Band we were able to come up with suggestions.

July

This was a very busy month for the Band. We had come a long way from our tentative beginnings. We played for an informal service at which our new Curate was welcomed. With the benefit of hindsight, I wonder what he thought of us! We were asked to play for an informal service on only five days notice by Alan, a very sympathetic but elderly member of the Methodist Congregation who would be leading the service. I normally turned down services at very short notice. As it turned out, Alan was very comfortable with working from our playlist. He was also open to our rather unusual ideas which included a Mexican Wave during the song "I believe in J. E. S. U. S."

We were asked to play for the blessing of a wedding. It was a second marriage for both husband and wife. There were four children from their previous marriages and it was a very child - centred, joyful ceremony. The elastic nature of the Band worked well as we were able to have two of the couple's children play recorders with us. They also played for "Here comes the Bride". It was a very special day. As a first for the Band, we were paid for playing which enabled us to invest in some flags and percussion instruments. These are still in use in our church 18 years later!

We were asked to play for another blessing – this time in the Methodist Church.

The only problem was a request to play "Everything I Do" by Bryan Adams from the film "Robin Hood". Given the content of the lyrics (which are secular but in tune with Christian principles) I was prepared to play it, but we had to find some playable music! We welcomed a new Band member in July, (Kathryn – a friend of my daughter, Elly). We also received confirmation from the Guinness Book of Records that our attempt was acceptable to them – provided we succeeded!

August

I managed to find the music for "Everything I Do" in the form of a rock score. All the parts of each instrument were written out fully – so it was a proper orchestra score. With some very concentrated practice we felt confident enough to play it at the blessing (our second one). My diary entry for the 5th August which was the day of the service reads;

"Mickey (our drummer) played beautifully (despite falling off his chair at one point)"

There was good feedback from the congregation (including some elderly people) which was very encouraging.

Our next event was to be playing on the Carnival Float which was being organized by the Church.

At this stage we had two more of Elly's friends wanting to join the Band and also the younger brother of our bass player, Mark, who was a very dedicated Band member. Sue and I prayed about whether we should run two bands so that we could split the ages. It was a difficult decision to make.

The older Band members were keen on forming their own band to be called "Powered by the Son". Sue and I were very positive about this as it meant we could concentrate on supporting our newer members. Also it meant sibling rivalry was less likely to be an issue. When Mark's brother, Alex, wanted to join the Band I asked him if he would fight with Mark. The answer was a resounding "Yes!"

We decided to carry on as were for the time being but encourage the "Powered by the Son" initiative.

Majestees (an excellent company that makes sweat shirts and t-shirts) had a logo with the name on. I wrote to them to ask if they would have a problem if that wording was used for a band name. They didn't, and so further progress was made.

We practiced through August for the Carnival, rehearsing a good cross section of songs including action songs. Sue made the biggest yellow flag I had ever seen, and by the end of August, we were ready.

September

The Carnival was on the 2nd September and to our relief the weather was good. We had seven Band members plus myself, Chris and Sue on the float and played for a good two hours. Tim had just got back from a holiday in America but came to join us on lead guitar despite a complete lack of sleep.

It was great to be able to witness to the whole village, although we had to blow up more balloons than you could imagine.

The rest of September consisted of serious rehearsing for “The Gift”, the plan being that this would take place in the Church in the village and involve as many people as possible. The last Sunday in September was the Christian Aid birthday party. We used some of the songs from Carnival Day to join in the celebrations.

October

There was a week of mission in the village. David Winter had been invited to attend the week. We felt very honoured to be asked to play at the main 11 o’clock service when he was preaching and thoroughly enjoyed the prestigious occasion. Although our song worked out we needed to be able to play through the church sound system to balance the instruments. We also needed a sound engineer. My heartfelt diary comment was “Help please, God!”

We played at a Women's Institute meeting, supporting members of our Village Youth Club and, the same week,we created our very own World Record. With the help of Paul, a sound engineer, who was an answer to a prayer, we completed the task in 3 hours 20 minutes. We were able to use the school hall and, in order to balance the sound, had to put the drum kit in the headmaster's study – and shut the door!

We had asked two people from the village to choose the bible verse for us so there was no question of any advance planning. They took the task very seriously and I soon felt we might have pushed ourselves too far with the challenge. We split into two groups to write a verse and a chorus. It was only when we put them together that we realized they sounded as if they came

from two different songs! Still, they were in the same key and the words were good.

Here they are:

BIBLE REFERENCE
Matthew Chapter 4 Verses 18 – 22

It was an ordinary day
The work was done
When a man said "fish again"
My nets were dry
But from his eye
I saw I must obey his word.

As I rowed I heard his word
The catch nearly overflowed
It was so clear
I filled with fear
Because I knew he was divine

But then he said "Don't be afraid,
And walk with me;
Become a fisher of men."
I left my wife,
My boat, my life,
To spread the Word to all I meet.

CODA

It was an ordinary day, just an ordinary day,
He changed my life – in every way
And now I'll never have another ordinary day
It was an ordinary day, just an ordinary day,
He changed my life – in every way
And now I'll never have another ordinary day

It was very encouraging to see all the Band members working together and resolving any differences between them. We did not have time for arguments.

The next problem was putting the music into the computer. We had a very limited music notation program. The computer seemed determined to be difficult. The Band members, especially Mark, were invaluable at this stage. The next step was practicing it together so we could play it to the congregation that was starting to arrive.

A full service had been planned to include our song. Fortunately, the congregation did arrive and the service did go ahead. The song was played and sung. Our final task was to sell at least 25 copies of either the sheet music or the cassette we had produced to different individuals. We sold the last one 3 hours 20 minutes after we started. The sense of elation was amazing and shared both by the Band and our village community. The local radio had sent an interviewer to talk to us which added to the significance of the day for the Band members.

As a celebration, we hired the local swimming pool and we took the Band there a week later and had a pool party. We took along tapes of Christian worship to put on the pool sound system and had a lot of fun. We wrote to the Bishop of the Diocese, David Stancliffe, sending him a copy of the World Record song and he wrote back.

The remainder of October and virtually all of November was taken up with rehearsals for "The Gift". There were eleven Band members taking part (in addition to me, Sue, Chris and Paul who had come on board as our sound engineer and bass guitar player, when needed)

"The Gift" consists of songs linked by prayers and readings. There is plenty of scope for adding suitable material. We wanted as many people as possible to join in with us.

Therefore, I asked some members of both the Anglican and Methodist congregations to help us. They were happy to act as narrators and to include dramatic readings. Church members were also willing to provide refreshments for the interval. We put together a choir, based around our church choir to do the singing and some people from a neighbouring church which was just outside our diocese came along to sing as well. We also invited the village hand bell ringers to join us and they played as the people arrived as well as during two of the songs.

For three of the songs we learned how to deaf sign them from a friend living in the village. We also asked a local ballet teacher and member of our congregation to choreograph dances for

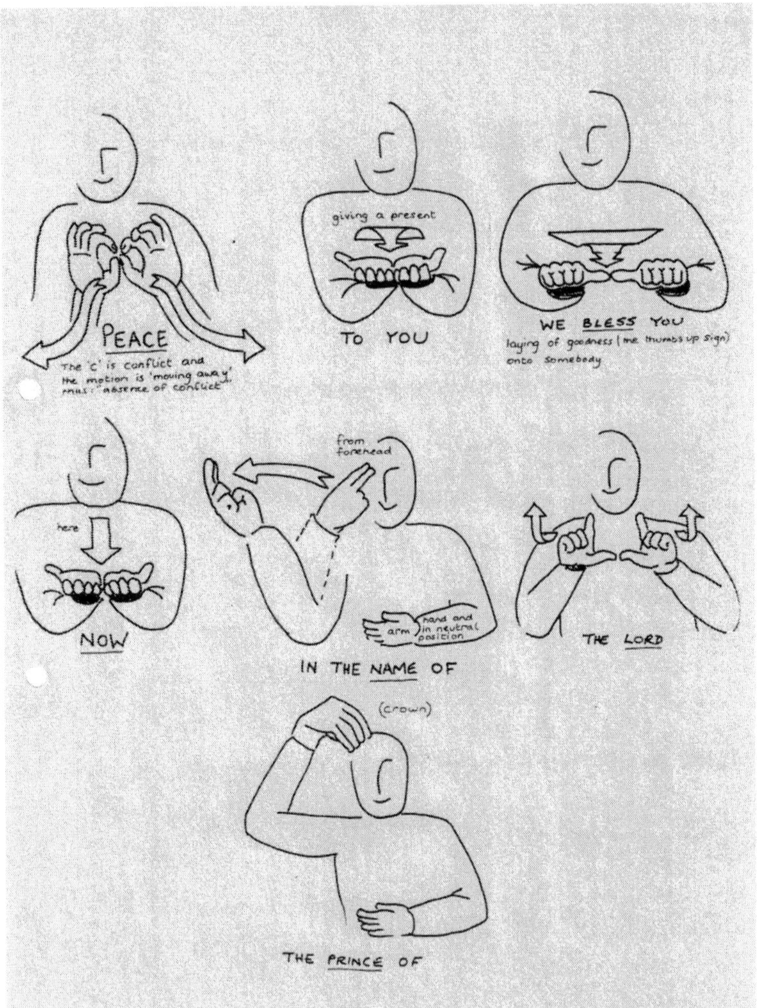

two of the pieces and we had children involved in those dances.

The Band was the basis for the music but we added two members of the adult worship group from the church which gave us an extra flautist and guitarist. There were two songs with a decidedly Hebrew flavor. There was a new adult member of our congregation who is a very talented violinist. He agreed to join us for those pieces. By the time we had added in these extra people we had a very good group. The Band was truly living up to its name – Elastic.

Our local village school is a church school. They joined in by spray painting fir cones silver and tying labels onto them with a Christmas message. Each person who came to watch (150 in all) received a fir cone to hang on their Christmas tree.

I had been very nervous in the weeks running up to the event as I had never undertaken anything like this before. It was our violinist who reassured me. His view was that as we were putting on the event to worship and honour God, then God would not allow anything to go wrong. I was not quite as certain since there are times when I feel God wants us to learn by adversity. However, on this occasion our violinist was right. The event was a great success. At the 11.00 am service the following day the church had a real buzz of excitement about it. The only criticism was that it should have been repeated the next day and then to other churches in the diocesan team. I had been so nervous before the event that I had been in tears after one service praying that people would come. To see the joy it created was more than I had dared to hope for.

It was back to reality the following Sunday. We played three songs from "The Gift" in the 11 am service but the church sound system was playing up. This was perceived as the Band's fault. Even though I knew it wasn't, we had to live with the criticism. On Christmas eve we played for the

Christingle Service. The sound system behaved itself and we ended the year on a good note – metaphorically as well as literally. One of the Christmas presents we received was a recording of "The Gift" – a wonderful present. My final words for the year in my diary were;

> "The Band can be justifiably proud of their work and grateful to God for their giftings"

Year Four

1996

January

We started again on the 9th January. The older members who had decided to form Powered by the Son were getting their t-shirts organized.

We discussed what else they would need to think about which clearly gave them pause for thought. The music we were practicing at this stage included "I will speak out", "As we are gathered", "Brother let me be your servant" (we worked out actions to this as well), "Restore O Lord", "Servant King" and "Jesus Stand Among Us"

I was in Salisbury working on the 10th January when I decided to call into the Diocesan Youth Office. I was aware of the All Night Youth Festival due to take place in Salisbury Cathedral on the 5th July. I had been thinking it might be possible for the Band to be involved, perhaps by running a workshop to encourage others. I talked to the Secretary who was interested to hear about what we were doing. Two days later I received a phone call asking if we would be willing to play on the main stage at 4 – 5 am and if we would play at an event designed to launch the Festival to take place a month earlier. Everyone in the Band was very excited with the news.

Normal Band life continued as well and we had to rehearse and then play for the Methodist service of Christian Unity. There were eight Band members playing in addition to Sue and me. The Band had the ability to bring lots of energy to these services which was really valued by the majority of the church attendees.

We were rehearsing in the Church as the School Room (where the plaster fell off the ceiling) was being renovated. The church was very cold in winter but there was plenty of space and it meant we got used to the acoustics.

There was still much debate about the best t-shirts for Powered by the Son. We had decided that they would play with the Elastic Band at the Launch. At the Festival each band would take a half hour slot.

Our last rehearsal in January was in a very cold church. One of the Band members was eager to let us know that his non-christian band had got a paying gig supported by a band called Hamsters from Hell. I did wonder if we'd gone wrong somewhere but decided it was better to leave it in God's hands.

February

Two rehearsals had to be cancelled because of snow. On the 9th February we played at our local youth club and a new person, Chris, appeared with his guitar. We welcomed him in and had an enjoyable very lively evening. I noticed that the boys at the youth club seemed to really enjoy practicing kick boxing moves. This prompted me to write a song about being strong if you want to follow Jesus. I have always been interested in learning about the power that Jesus is able to command. The songs about Jesus being meek and mild did not ring true for me. The song proved popular with the boys and a significant number of the girls.

We put together a sketch to include in our set at the All Night Youth Festival. The idea was to show a Parochial Church Council meeting at which a group of young people would encourage the PCC (with the help of Old Testament quotations) to consider using a youth band for an important service. The tone of the sketch was very light hearted but it made a serious point.

We started reading it through at the February rehearsals to see if it could work. The Band members were enthusiastic about it. By now (nearly 4 years into the life of the Band) we had got to know each other well. Two of the boys (Mark and Tim) came to my house to record one of Mark's songs on our new 4-track recorder and we all had a good time.

The rehearsals included songs such as Eric Clapton's "Tears in Heaven" which Eric wrote after the death of his son.

March

A very important part of our work with the Band was acting as communicators between the younger Band members and the older members of the congregations, both Anglican and Methodist. The people leading some of the services were in their 60's and 70's. They were extremely positive about involving the young people but didn't always understand how they could be used. I have a diary entry from this time saying that I had been explaining who Eric Clapton was and what a cover was to a group of elderly worship leaders.

It was in March that we supported the Youth Club Talent show by playing some lively Christian songs (eg "Ho – Ho – Holy Spirit"). We also played for an informal service at the Methodists. According to my notes, it was loud but well received. By now our older members were very keen to get going with their band Powered by the Son and we were keen to encourage them.

The following week Sue and I went to a meeting at a free church in another village (Ashbury) where there was to be prayer for youthwork. We talked about the Elastic Band and Powered by the Son and were offered a gig.

On the 24th March we held an Elastic Band workshop but the PBTS members turned up as well! They were keen to talk about what they wanted to wear for gigs so we talked about that and the forthcoming Launch and Festival in Salisbury.

April

This was a very busy month rehearsing seriously for Salisbury. It was very good to have such a clear focus. The Launch date was looming (18th May 1996 – three years less a week from our very first session)

May

We managed to fit in an informal service before the Launch. People were still talking about "The Gift" from December and asking if we were doing it again. I had to say no, as the work involved had been so great. We kept our focus on the Band and the Launch. At the final rehearsal we had 14 Band members plus Sue, myself, Chris my husband and Paul, a friend of ours who had experience of playing in bands and sound engineering. He had helped us by running the sound desk right the way through to the time the Band came to an end.

The Launch was in Salisbury (about an hour's drive away) and so there were travelling logistics to work out. It was attended by the Bishop of Salisbury and there were youth workers there from around the Diocese.

Four parents of Band members came to help with transport and were favourably impressed with what the Band were able to do. We played an Elastic Band set and then Powered by the Son played their own set. The Launch went well and gave us encouragement for the Festival proper in July.

We went for a burger afterwards and this became a Band ritual after each gig that was away from home. It was a wonderful time to chat and share happy memories.

It was at this time that I took the visual side of the Band more seriously. I found a person on Bristol Market who was very gifted at making air brushed t-shirts. I explained what I wanted and within a couple of minutes he sketched an Elastic Band

man which he used to create very smart t-shirts. He could customize them for each instrument and they proved extremely popular. The t-shirt on the front of this book shows a bass player. My t-shirt showed a keyboard player.

June

There were more rehearsals including (on the 18th June) when England were playing Scotland at football. Rather than miss the rehearsal, a band member decided to come, but bring his walkman to listen to the match. Needless to say, the music sounded grim. I tried to stay positive. Sue was on holiday as well which meant we were missing her invaluable input. This was the month that we found out our World Record attempt had been recognized by the Guinness Book of Records, which was great news and further encouragement.

We organized a run-through with audience in the church and, five days later, a run-through at the youth club. Both of these were well received and it was good to see the interest shown by non-Band members, particularly with the deaf signing for three of the songs.

On the 30th June there was a service of ordination in the church in the next village, the first for 900 years. The person being ordained, Paul (not our sound engineer) had rashly agreed to take part in the sketch we were taking to the Salisbury Festival and so we had got to know him quite well. We felt very honoured that he wanted us to play, deaf sign and use ribbons on some of the songs at the service. It was a very memorable service. Paul was pleased we were there. It was a very full service with a great deal of variety. We were at the most extrovert end and it seemed to me that some of the congregation had not experienced our colourful and energetic style of worship. We did not hear any adverse comments but it was one of those times when I needed to believe that we were doing what God wanted us to do.

July

This was an extraordinary month. The All Night Youth Festival in Salisbury Cathedral was on the 5th July. We travelled in groups and arrived mid-afternoon. This gave us plenty of time to get there and work out what we were doing and where. The other mainstage bands included DBA, Gethsemane Rose and Why?. They had their own CDs for sale and were used to playing at mainstream Christian festivals.

I was thrilled to see how they interacted with our Band members, treating them as other musicians in their own right. It was a real confidence boost for all of us. We were unable to have a sound check as that would have interfered with Evensong. This put a great deal of responsibility onto Paul, our sound man, to correct any problems very quickly once we started playing.

Before the Festival we had come up with the idea of signing real elastic bands and running a competition at the Festival to see who could collect the largest number of elastic bands by coming up to us and asking us for one. This meant we were being recognized by our t-shirts and we were raising awareness. I was intrigued when the Bishop of Salisbury showed me his collection of bands by rolling up his purple sleeve!

As the Festival got under way we enjoyed listening to the other bands and some of us got some sleep. At 3.45 am we were ready to go…..

Our set lasted an hour in total including the sketch, and for the last 20 minutes Powered by the Son had the stage to themselves.

As I played the final notes of "Peace to you" the sun was rising and rays of multicoloured light came streaming through the stained glass windows of that magnificent Cathedral onto my keyboard.

It was and remains the most special moment of my spiritual journey.

There was a service in the morning to end the Festival and then we came back home – exhausted and elated. We had received great support from some of the parents of the band members who had been able to join us. Within 4 days we were able to watch a video and have a debrief. It was a really fun evening – we heard classic pieces of advice such as “Don’t head bang with your bag on”

We wanted to carry on meeting through the summer and decided to turn our hands to song writing. We held the sessions at our house and had one at Sue’s house. We had seven Band members attending each session, including a Polish exchange student who was staying with a member of our congregation. On the 16th July we had different songs being written in each room of our house at the same time, including one in Polish! It was a really creative and blessed evening.

Sue, Paul, Chris and I went to the Soul Survivor Festival during July which gave us some useful “down time” and we met Duncan from the Toybox Charity.

As a result, Chris, Paul and I wrote a song about the problems facing children and young people in Guatemala. It made me realize how many opportunities our young people have. However, the challenges they face are just as real for them.

August

We spent August rehearsing and we managed to send off some entries to the Diocesan song writing competition. These were the songs the band members had written in July. We spent part of one session teaching Band members how to put up music and microphone stands. At least, we thought, it might speed things up when we arrived for a service or rehearsal. It seemed to be the kind of job nobody else wanted to do.

September

We were back up to full strength after the summer holidays. We had an informal service to play for in Ramsbury at the end of the month. The songs we were playing included "We have called on you Lord", "More love, more power" (a real Band favourite), "Great is the Lord" and "God who made the sea and sky" We wrote prayers which were said over the music to "More love, More power" in between the verses. This worked very well.

We were able to share our photos from the All Night Festival which had come out well. As a result of playing at the Launch, we received an invitation to visit a Baptist church in Trowbridge and stay over on Saturday night. This was going to be a completely new experience for us.

October

The whole of October was taken up with planning and rehearsing for Trowbridge. There was to be a party on Saturday night and we were playing for their service on Sunday. Various members of their congregation were providing accommodation for Saturday night. There was a lot of planning to do and also real excitement at the prospect of being the visiting band. The plan was that this trip would not involve Powered by the Son but would be a good opportunity to develop the younger members we now had. There were seven young people going to Trowbridge but of those, only one had been with us from our start in May 1993.

November

The Trowbridge weekend took place on the first weekend in November. It was a very enjoyable weekend and good experience for our band members who were welcomed whole heartedly. I was particularly pleased that, because of the elastic nature of our band, we were able to include young people from the Trowbridge church in the band at the Sunday morning service. This included a boy with learning difficulties who had a specially adapted guitar. We bumped into him at Spring Harvest a couple of years later and had a very special reunion.

The rest of November was taken up with practices for our next "bright idea". We had decided to try to raise money for "Children in Need" by inviting people to a fund raising event. We would play the first 6 – 8 bars of 57 different Christian songs one after another. The audience had to name as many of the songs as possible. They paid to enter and there was a prize for the person who got the most right. It was a nightmare organizing the music but great fun playing it. We managed to play all the songs and a very musical audience member got 53 right. Nearly £300 was raised and we had a real sense of fellowship over working together.

The last November rehearsal saw us starting to practice for the Christingle service. This is a major service in our village and my concern was that the expectations of the congregation were now very high when the Band was playing. However, the line up of Band members was completely different from 6 months previously

December

The Band line up was now Sue, Chris, Paul and me and eleven Band members all of whom had joined within the last year. We were seeing the "Elastic" principle in practice. As this group had not had the equivalent of the British Youth for

Christ "Just Looking" course we decided to use the "Youth Alpha" material during the sessions. Some of our members did not attend church, nor did their parents, so we felt it was important to have a Christian framework. We were also keen to introduce the Band members to other Christian role models. We always felt completely inadequate in that role and so Sue brought along a video about Christians in Sport which was very popular.

The Christingle service went ahead on the 24th December. There was a lot of tinsel, Sue and I were wearing reindeer antlers and the keyboard was dressed up with a full set of fairy lights.

There was one scary moment when a non-band member kicked out one lead and cut all the power but Paul sorted it out very quickly. It was a good service to finish our exciting year.

Following is our Annual Review with some additional material from the All Night Festival. The original has been scanned in. This may make some of the words difficult to read but I hope you will be able to see what the Annual Report really looked like.

Only copy - please do not remove.
THE ELASTIC BAND
RETROSPECTIVE
'96

1996 AND ALL THAT

Its that time of year again. Youve cleaned the reindeer droppings off the carpet (the ones the cat didnt eat anyway)* watched Tim and Mark rescue the church from certain destruction by fire at the Christingle service and reflected again on the mystery of Gods coming into this world in human flesh (these are not necessarily in order of importance!

Its time to open up the diary and reflect on an action packed Elastic Band Year. Here you will read of the successes and the failures the fun and the sadness. In fact everything that goes to make up an amazing experience for a lot of people (and thats just the congregations).

So here we go with the highlights

JANUARY
Discussions commence about a breakaway Band to be called Powered by the Son. Russell accuses Ros of abandoning the Band! (Liam Gallagher eat your heart out - it happened here first).Mark said he wanted to write Christian songs to tell people about Jesus using contemporary music!

I talk our way into the Salisbury Festival.

Mark has his first paying gig supporting Hamsters From Hell!

FEBRUARY
We gig at the youth club and Chris Spath joins us. I realise its time to write a song about being Strong to follow Jesus. Ive just about had it with the meekness and mildness.

We gave the Salisbury script its first run through. The band improved on it immediately.

Mark cried when his guitar string snapped. (aaaaaaaaaaaaaah)

MARCH
I explain to the church elders who Eric Clapton is and what a cover is.Powered By the Son sweatshirts and my four track arrive. We play at the Youth Club Talent show and Chris realises that if you are singing you really have to start in the same key as the instrumentalists!

Mickey's Band came first at the Marlborough Brass Band contest.

Tim gets into top gear with PBTS(Powered By the Son) and invitations are sent out to join (not that IIIIIIIIIIIIIIIIII got one of course!).

APRIL
Salisbury rehearsals start in earnest. Its a long hard slog

MAY
We now have the deaf signs as well. We play for the Launch of the Festival in Salisbury and the Bishop joins in with the action songs. We have a trip out to Burger King afterwards.The new

Elastic Band T shirts arrive especially customised for us.

JUNE
Lots more rehearsals. There was a grim one when the guitarists had walkmans on to listen to the football but otherwise we were getting there.

We get written confirmation we are in the Guiness Book Of Records Files.

We are told that we are the only Band on mainstage at the Festival who dont get a sound check!!!!!!!!!!!!!!!!!!!!

JULY
The Alive Festival.See write up elsewhere.

We start on song writing both for ourselves and the Diocese competition.We have some excellent sessions at 17 Kandahar with different songs being written in every room and with one in Polish!

We go to the Soul Survivors Festival and make connections with the Cross Rhythms Festival organisers.

AUGUST
The entries for the competition are sent off after I spend hours putting them on the computer then we do a decent recording of two of them.

SEPTEMBER
Our numbers are growing and in true Elastic Band fashion the line up looks totally different from the way it looked in July!

Mickey started work.We played for an Informal service in Ramsbury. It was good but freezing cold!

OCTOBER
We now have a lovely warm kitchen to rehearse in as well. Thank you for Laura and Matthew. We hope to see Chris Spath's saxophone sometime!

NOVEMBER
An amazing sleepover in Trowbridge. See separate write up. Tim Newman is now an honorary band member!

Children in Need - we raise over £300!!!!!!!!!!!!!!!!
We go to Burgerking in Salisbury after the prize giving in the Cathedral as Elly has come second in the under 13s section with her song Trusting in God!

DECEMBER
Christingle. Paul sprints into action when a power lead is pulled by a non band member. Ros wears reindeer antlers. Russell has fairy lights on his and Ros's keyboard. We are talking serious tinsel here! The candle lit church is a beautiful reminder to all of us why we are here why we worship God and why the Elastic Band will continue and flourish - Because Jesus was born on earth and died for us.

ALIVE - ALL NIGHT YOUTH FESTIVAL

For once even Im lost for words to describe this amazing event of which we were a part (you will notice that my grammar remains impeccable!). I think the best idea is to start at the beginning and then keep going! It all really started when Sue and I attended the Pebble in the Pond Youth Leader Conference in Salisbury and were told that there was to be an all night festival in the Cathedral and we might be able to get involved.

Being gluttons for punishment we said that we did want to be involved and wrote and told them so. We then wrote again as we hadnt heard anything and I called in at the Diocesan Office in January 1996 when we still hadnt heard anything. Finding the office was quite an achievement and I banged hard and pressed bells on three different doors before finding my way in. I then met Jill who is utterly wonderful and I talked and talked and talked (so whats new?) until she agreed to put forward the Elastic Band for inclusion in the Festival. I made it clear that we would be willing to play on the smallest stage (that was because I hadnt asked Mark s opinion first) and we would play at four in the morning if need be (so yes it was all MY FAULT). By the end of the conversation I felt that we were in with a chance of at least something. As the final decisions were being made that week it was definitely a God sent opportunity for me to talk to Jill. By lunchtime the following Friday we found out that we were to be on the main stage and we were to be invited to play at the launch of the Festival in May. I immediately went into "Oh No what have I let us in for mode"........................

However Sue was very supportive with comments like "Oh No what have you let us in for" and she promptly started polishing her flag ready for the big days!I decided early on that we needed to have something important to contribute apart from our immense talent so I wrote a sketch with some audience interaction for us to perform and asked Jan Addis if she would be willing to work out deaf signing for the songs we intended to do. So there followed months of preparation whilst we worked on the sketch , on music for the Launch on learning the signing and on finding the right costumes and props for the sketch.

As always there were lots of special moments. The first read through of the sketch was excellent. Especially when Mark came out with "Praise Him with THE CLASH" leaving someone else with the immortal words "........ of cymbals". I knew then that the sketch would work.At the launch we realised that we could lead worship and even after the organisers had heard us we were still going to be on the main stage! The rehearsals as always were good bad and indifferent and we made the spectacular discovery that rehearsing whilst listening to England playing Holland on ones walkman affects the ability to play quite dramatically (4-1 if you really want to know). It was very difficult to have everyone at every rehearsal and for some of them we used substitutes. Russell played every part in the sketch at various different stages only really drawing the line at wearing a skirt to play Sue s part. No not even a long skirt!!!!

We found that as the rehearsals continued more and more young people came along to watch and BE INTERVIEWED by our roving or raving reporter. This was good practice for him. What would you say to the person who wants to wear a batman costume in church "Ever thought of the Ministry ?". And we made the important discovery that if you shake up a bottle of fizzy drink and explode it on the floor you can cover not just the sound man and the sound desk but half the carpet as well! Well you live and learn. We invited audiences along and played at the youth club so that we would be very well rehearsed and I am sure that paid off.

The launch went very well indeed and gave us the courage to keep going. We were delighted that the bishop joined in with our action song and Sue didnt kill anyone with her flag although I noticed several people giving her a little more respect after they had seen it in action! We were then on the run down to the Festival itself. We started to hit problems. I was told that out of all the bands on the main stage we were not to be allowed a sound check because Evensong and a choir practice in the Cathedral had to go ahead and that took up the time for our sound check. I received this news just before having lunch with our vicar and he was treated to me launching into how unfair and unreasonable it all was (not a pretty sight). He took it very well. Our sound man said he would speak nicely to the sound company and Chris launched a pincer movement by speaking to Jill. By this stage the week before the Festival Jill was tearing her hair out and it was now down to Paul with more experience than the rest of us put together to get us out of this particular nightmare. In true Paul fashion he took control and sorted out when we had to arrive how to get the instruments there how to speak to sound people and how to speak to other bands. Without him we would not have survived.

The sound checks began at 12.00 noon and went straight through to 5.00 p.m.without a break and without a space for us. Evensong started at 5.00 p.m.We arrived between 12.30 at 2.00 a.m. and with some very skilful discussions by Paul with the sound desk we managed to get on for our sound check at 4.00 p.m. and within half an hour I knew that it was going to be O.K. I had felt very apprehensive on arrival.The stage looked enormous with the lighting on scaffolding and Gethsemane Rose were filling the Cathedral with heavy rock much to the consternation of the ladies from the volunteer team on duty that day.However once the band were on stage I realised that we could genuinely hold our own.

We also had time to talk to the other bands and discuss such theological points as "Is it o.k.to play frisbee in the Cathedral during Evensong provided the frisbee doesnt hit the floor? Yes to that one.And "Where did you get your t shirts from?" That was Gethsemane Rose asking us incidentally! We then went to explore the tea shops of Salisbury and eat cake and apple strudel and do other heavy metal type things (not).

We then came back to welcome the younger members of the band who had to miss the sound check as they were at school and to welcome our helpers and supporters. It was great to see lots of familiar faces and to know that even people older than me (WOW) were prepared to stay up all night to support us. We then started to be able to enjoy the Festival and head bang to Gethsemane Rose jig to Why and try to sleep (ha) any chance that appeared. The Bishop opened the Festival and held a short service at midnight. We hung around in the hospitality trying to find famous other band members to talk to and rehearsing like mad so that we wouldnt forget our lines. We had decided that to generate interest in the band we would run a competition for people to collect elastic bands that band members had signed beforehand with a trophy for the person who collected the most. A real treat for me was to see that even the Bishop was collecting them! He rolled up his very impressive purple sleeve just to show me! He did only have five though so I felt he was unlikely to win.

As the evening wore on I realised that we were going to be on even later that 3.00 a.m. as the stage was running late. We had everyone ready for 2.30 a.m. anyway and then had to keep up the momentum and energy for two hours. This was not easy and I just hoped and prayed that the adrenalin would do the trick. We also had a chance to pray to focus us on what we were about to do and then we were on. The next hour is now just a blur of excitement of real pleasure and of joy at seeing the signing starting to work as we were able to really communicate with the people there. It was a real privilege. I was able to see Powered By The Son in all their glory and talk to the Bishop about just how much the young people have to offer.

Afterwards it was a time of letting down and letting go. Of knowing that we had been there and done it. A few of us stayed on for the end of the Festival and the Eucharist Service where the Bishop anointed the youth workers there and with Paul Trickey's invaluable help I managed to get to my feet to go forward with everyone else. For the communion even he couldnt get me on my feet so he organised a flying eucharist server to come to my chair. He gets my steward of the year award!

So somehow we all arrived safely home and slept as much as possible with the exception of Paul and Tim and Sarah who were going on to other events. I slept through My Fair Lady on video and woke up in my lounge at noon on Saturday wondering if it had all be a dream. It wasnt - it was an amazing experience.

SONG WRITING AND THE ELASTIC BAND

1996 gave the Band the opportunity to have a go at song writing.The Diocesan Hymn writing competition gave us the incentive but the results of the song writing have extended beyond the competition itself. Here is a list of the entries we put in.

1. Celebration Express by Ros and Chris
2. The Creed by Ros
3. Come Lord into my life by Alex
4. God Who Made The Sky And Sea by Elly and Kathryn
5. In Seven Nights And Days by Tabitha Jodie and Elizabeth
6. Trusting In God by Elly
7. God Loves You by Kathryn

We were absolutely delighted that a Band Member won a prize as Elly came second in the under 13 group and Elly Lizzie and Laura were able to attend the prize giving in Salisbury. However what the song writing has done for the Band is to expand our repertoire to include some of these new songs and you will all be familiar by now with God Who Made The Sky and Sea. I hope there will be more song writing opportunities in the future as there is a lot of potential out there. We did think that you would like to hear from Elly as a result of her success so your intrepid reporters Sue and Ros tried to interview her whilst she was watching T.V. Judge the result for yourself!

1.What is your favourite food? Roast and chips
2.What is your favourite sport? Gymnastics and riding
3.What is the most embarassing thing that has ever happened to you? (This interview took place before her father went out on a bike ride with her with his reindeer antlers on) Having a father as a pantomime Dame (I think you could relate to that one Matthew!)
4.What is the biggest audience you have ever played to? 2500
5.And the smallest? 4
6.BBC or ITV? BBC
7.Football or Rugby? Football
8.What did you think of the prize giving ceremony in the Cathedral? It was freezing cold
9.What did you think of the secondary prize giving ceremony in Burger King afterwards? It was much better
10.How did you come to write your prize winning song?
I had to because I am in the Elastic Band (Actually it was COMPLETELY VOLUNTARY and anyway living on bread and water for three months wouldnt have done her much harm at all!)
11.What is the worst thing about your song? The music - its so boring
12.What is your ambition? To become a teacher fly around the world and get to grade 8 on the flute
13.Coke or Pepsi? Pepsi

So there you have it - the incisive and slick interview technique of Sue and Ros for all to see.

ELASTIC BAND MEMBERSHIP 1996

We have had a very extensive line up this year and of course some of the people are now Powered By The Son (although I like to think we are all powered by the Son in our own little way!) so I have tried to identify those people as well with some clever initials! You'll never guess what they mean. I've also put the instruments down that have been played but not against the correct people so you can have fun drawing lines all over the page to connect the correct person to the correct instruments or instrument as the case may be (sad isnt it!).

Mark (PTTM)
Tim (PTTM)
Russell (PTTM)
Sarah (PTTM)
Louisa (PTTM)
Sally (PTTM)
Mickey (PTTM)
Kirsty (PALTTM)
Chris
Laura

Elly
Kathryn
Elizabeth
Laura
Matthew

Pete
Matthew
Alex
Alex
Sue
Chris
Paul
Ros
Tim (Newman)
Tabitha
Jodie

keyboards
flute
rhythm guitar
lead guitar
bass guitar
drum kit
violin
tambourine
clarinet
large yellow and potentially lethal flag
bells
tenor recorder
another violin
even bigger keyboard
a keyboard you can stack on top of the first keyboard
synth module
descant recorder
cazoo (AAAAAAAAAAAAAAAAAAAAAH)
pitch pipe
bodhran
vocals
more vocals
even more vocals
ribbons
deaf signing
hand clapping

Honorary adults this year are
Mike Walters for being prepared to sit next to someone wearing a plastic rain hat
Peter Lawler for being brave enough to wave his stick at Mark and Mickey for playing too loudly (I've been wanting to do that for years!)
Paul Kingman for letting us be a part of his ordination
Lucy Bowers for telling us all so convincingly we can worship and enjoy ourselves (and how right she is!)

ELASTIC BAND 1996 GIG LIST

21st January Methodist Church Service of Christian Unity

9th February Methodist Hall Youth Club

11th February Workshop and Informal Service

8th March Youth Club Talent Show

10th March Workshop and Informal Service

24th March Workshop and Informal Service

12th May Informal Service and Workshop

18th May Launch of the Alive Festival in Salisbury

28th June Run through for Salisbury at the Youth Club

30th June Paul Kingman's ordination at Ramsbury

5th July Salisbury Cathedral Alive Festival

29th September Ramsbury Informal Service

27th October Informal Service

2/3rd November Praise Party and Family Service in Trowbridge

24th November Children in Need event in St Michaels School

24th December Christingle Service at St Michaels

ELASTIC BAND PRIZE QUIZ 1996

For the first (and probably the only) time in living memory this retrospective contains a prize quiz. If anyone gets all the answers write and written down and spelt properly in nice joined up writing! they will win a valuable prize to be chosen from the following:-

1 A subscription to Crossrhythms
2 An Ishmael tape or C.D.
3 A Kendrick tape or C.D. (Kendrick who?)

So get your thinking caps on!

1. Who said "Kendrick Who?" and where did they say it?
2. Who cried when his guitar string broke?
3. How many musicians did King David have?
4. Who said "I unfortunately had to admit there must be a God" when Skellig were late for their sound check?
5. Who asked who if it was O.K. to play Frisbee during Evensong?
6. Who did we think we had lost at Salisbury and where was he?
7. How much money did we raise for Chidren in Need?
8. Who had the largest number of correctly identified songs at the Children in Need event and how many did he/she correctly identify?
9. What item of food is referred to when describing the deaf signs for Peace To You?
10. Whose ordination did we play for in 1996?
11. Who beat who at football and what was the final score on the 18th June during an Elastic Band rehearsal though fortunately they were not actually playing football in the church!?
12. Who bought a big new keyboard in 1996?
13. Who sprayed a fizzy drink all over the church during an Elastic Band rehearsal?
14. Who saved the church from destruction by fire in 1996?
15. Who said "It'll sound really good once you've got the order right" after I had spent eleven hours getting the order right and have his scars healed yet?
16. Whose tooth fell out seconds before we went on stage at Salisbury?
17. Who said "Dont head bang with your bag on"?
18. Who gave the sound advice "Dont pick the fastest song for the sound check"?
19. Who said "Even 10 year olds can crowd surf"?
20. Who said "You can get away with wearing ripped jeans and leggings in a Cathedral"?
21. Who was wearing the ripped jeans and leggings in the first place?
22. Who said "Dont leave Festivals too early cos your parents will still be asleep"?
23. Who said "Dont jump off stages cos it hurts your ankles"?
24. Which honorary member of the Band lives in Trowbridge?
25. Which verse in which psalm is the inspiration for the Band?
26. Which famous Christian sports people were on the video Sue brought along fro us to watch at Matthew and Laura's?
27. What is the difference in degrees centigrade between the temperature in Laura and Matthew's kitchen and St Michael's church on an average December evening at 9.00 p.m.?
28. Did you feel the mountains tremble and if so when?

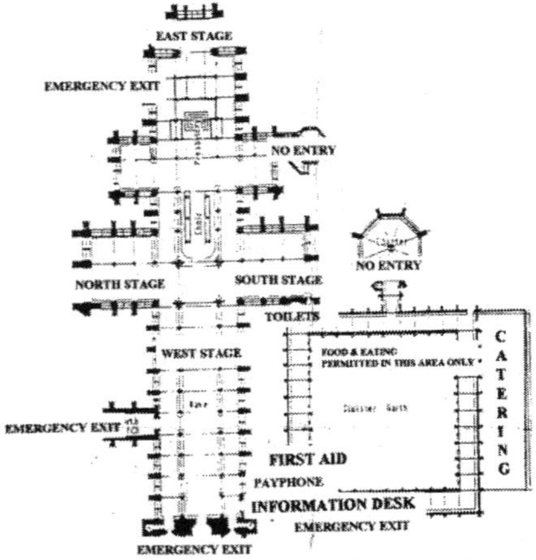

Our special thanks go to the following people and organisations, without whose help there would be no festival:
WILTSHIRE COUNTY COUNCIL YOUTH SERVICE
DORSET COUNTY COUNCIL YOUTH SERVICE
THE WIMBORNE EDUCATIONAL TRUST
THE JERUSALEM TRUST
SHERBORNE ABBEY FAITH IN ACTION COMMITTEE
J B ALLEN TRUST
THE DIOCESAN BOARD OF EDUCATION
RT REVD DAVID STANCLIFFE, THE LORD BISHOP OF SALISBURY

SALISBURY DIOCESE

5 JULY 1996

ALIVE

ALL-NIGHT FESTIVAL

"In Christ shall all be made alive"
I Corinthians 15 v 22

PROGRAMME

TIMETABLE

The event has been organised around four stages, running almost continuously throughout the night, providing a wide variety of music, performances and workshops. You are invited to move around the stages as you feel you would like, to join in with what is going on, or just sit and watch. During the twelve hours of the festival we hope to take you on a spiritual journey of discovery.

	WEST STAGE	EAST STAGE	NORTH STAGE	SOUTH STAGE
8.00pm	OPENING AND WELCOME BY THE BISHOP			
8.10pm	GETHSEMANE ROSE	WORSHIP The Other Guests	'Playing God' C.Y.F.A.	
9.05pm		SUNRISE DISCO	Tale-Ann Hilton presents 'Twelve'	FRESH CLAIM
10.00pm	EDEN BURNING		'Partners with The Poor' World Vision	Diocesan Youth Adviser - workshops for leaders
11.00pm	WHY?	'Who Runs the World?' Christian Aid	ROCKHOUSE	'Called To Learn' Crisis
Midnight	THE BISHOP ADDRESSES THE WHOLE EVENT			
12.10am	SKELLIG	'The Snake & the Ladder' Jakes Ladder Theater Company	'To Daddy Go or Stay' C.M.S.	Melksham Christian Fellowship
1.05am	Barn Dance	What 4 Rolling Magazine	'The Titanic Brothers' Drama, and writing	
2.00am	dba	Snap Christian Drama Group	'Actions Speak' Viz-a-Viz multi media roadshow	
3.00am	ELASTIC BAND POWERED BY THE SUN	LITTLE JAM	THE AMERICANS	'How You Can Help' Crisis
4.00am	Sound Foundation	Spanish Guitarist Jason Carter		First Aid Training
5.00am		TAIZE WORSHIP	'The Ultimate Africa Experience'	Frontier Youth Trust
6.00am	Bishop David	Sunrise Dance	'Beyond These Shores' Wycliffe Bible Translators	'Fully ALIVE - A Life to be lived' Crusaders
7.00am	EUCHARIST			
8.00am	Close			

- **Music of all styles and to suit everyone's tastes.** Big bands like Gethsemane Rose, Eden Burning, Why, Skellig, Fresh Claim and dba. Plus exciting music groups from our own Diocese - Rockhouse, Little Jam and the Elastic Band
- **Classical music** from Spanish Guitarist, Jason Carter
- **Dance music** from Sunrise and The Sound Foundation
- **The Barn Dance**
- **Workshops and Performances** from Christian Aid, C.Y.F.A., World Vision, CMS, Crisis, Mid African Ministry, Wycliffe Bible Translators, Melksham Christian Fellowship, Frontier Youth Trust and Crusaders
- **Drama** with Jakes Ladder Theatre Company, the Bible Society and Snap Christian Drama Group
- **Multi-media presentations** from Viz-a-Viz and What 4.
- **Art** with our resident sculpture Paul Hobbs and in our arts workshops
- **Worship** with The Other Guests and Taize style, as well as in our final Eucharist
- **Clowning** with Peter Cole in the Cathedral

Bishop David, the Bishop of Salisbury, will lead us in worship at the start, at midnight and in the closing Eucharist. He will be with us all night so do take the opportunity to chat with him.

Other Useful Information:

Information Desk - Is situated near the West Door (see map) and will be manned at all times. There is an emergency telephone located here but it should be noted that all non emergency calls should be made from the payphone near the restaurant.

First Aid - Is located at the Information Desk (see map) and will be manned throughout the event. Please find a steward to help you.

Catering - This year Angel Catering have agreed to provide us with hot food and drink throughout the night and will be based in the works yard (see map).

Stewards - ARE ALL VOLUNTEERS - so please respect and obey them, especially in the event of an emergency.

Display & Sales Areas - Shown on the map. You are welcome to add details of your own events to the display boards.

5 JULY 1996

ALIVE

ALL-NIGHT YOUTH FESTIVAL

YOUTH TEAM
SALISBURY DIOCESAN BOARD OF EDUCATION
AUDLEY HOUSE
CRANE STREET
SALISBURY
WILTS SP1 2QA

Telephone 01722 411977
Fax 01722 411990

	Time	West Stage	East Stage	North Stage	South Stage	Additional	Cathedral	Hospitality
1								
2	8.00pm	Event Starts	Opening & Welcome					
3	8.10pm	Gethsemane Rose	Isasic Ensemble - (Heather Waldeax)	C.Y.P.A.	Space			
4	9.05pm	Space for time overruns and stage changes etc	Offer to The Sound Foundation	Bible Society - Julie-Ann Hamilton presents 'Twelve'	Fresh Claim	Clowning Peter Cole	This area for art/ pottery/ painting etc	Hospitality offered in Wren Hall
5	10.00pm	Eden Burning	Dance for Christ	World Vision - 'Partners with the Door' - Working for Justice for the Third World	PN talk to youth leaders			
6	11.00pm	Why	Christian Aid - Robert Pearce	Gary Naylor - Rockhouse	Crisis - 'Who is Homeless'	Artist in Residence - Paul Hobbs, Sculpture- To work in far and from West Door and mount static display in Morning Chapel		
7	12 midnight	The Bishop						
8	12.10pm	Skellig	Jakes Ladder - drama workshop	C.M.S. - To Boldly Go or Stay	Melksham Christian Fellowship - Chris Gibb			
9	1.05am	Barn Dance (David Slater)	MAF - Dave Barker National Youth Director	Dave Hopwood - Drama - Acting Up 'Louder Than Words'	Clear space for time overruns	Franciscan Brothers share with young people		
10	2.00am	dBA	Andy Walker, Snap Christian Drama Group.	Tear Fund Viz-a-Viz roadshow Actions Speak	as above			
11	3.00am	Christian Music Dance Party	Emmanuel Band - Revd Paul Finch- Little Jam	Crisis - 'Who is Homeless'	Dance For Christ - Mary & Mark Fleeson			
12	4.00am	Ros Oswald - the Elastic Band/Powered by the Sun	Jason Carter - Spanish guitarist	space	Space			
13	5.00am	Clear Space for time overruns until 5.30am	Taize Worship PC Alan Knott	C.M.S. Mid African Ministry - Liz Kneebone - 'The Ultimate African Experience'	Frontier Youth Trust Ankle Ball			
14	6.00am	5.30am Bishop's Confirmation Preparation	Offer to The Sound Foundation	Wycliffe Bible - Beyond These Shores	Crusaders - Ian Macdonald - 'Fully ALIVE - A Life to be Lived'			
15	7.00am	EUCHARIST						
16	8.00am	CLOSE						

A WEEK IN THE LIFE OF AN ELASTIC BAND ORGANISER

Saturday : Stayed in whilst the family went to the Mop Fair to virtuously type out the information sheet for the Trowbridge gig. Tried to watch Casualty on T.V. at the same time and then realised that I had put Alex down to play violin on Heaven Invites You To A Party . Some party that would be! Switch off T. V. and feel virtuous and martyred at the same time. Remember sin of pride and have to repent quickly before pressing on. Put on spell check. Go to bed.

Sunday : Leap out of bed. Decide to wear Elastic Band T shirt to Sunday School. This is purely to demonstrate the significance of a good visual presentation and IS NOT because I just like wearing the T shirt. (repent again). Ask drummer if he will actually take his elastic band newsletter home if I give it to him now. He says no. Give it to his father in desperation as anxious to avoid trekking round village delivering said newsletters. Disturbed whilst eating delicious meal cooked by long suffering husband and rhythm guitarist (actually he has recently bought himself a 12 string so he isnt THAT long suffering) to give tape to ex elastic band bass player. Try to convince him that his own composition makes Paul Simon sound like a real amateur - not sure if I actually succeeded there. Ring Hazel who is out at HTB to ask for the address of MAYC so I can enter said brill song in their song writing competition. Am told that Hazel is at falling down church rather than falling down hostelry in village. Am asked to ring back after 10 p.m. No good to me as all self respecting elastic band organisers collapse exhausted into bed at about 9.30 p.m. even when they havent been running a rehearsal. Spend time improvising on the piano as the funeral I went to the previous day is still very much with me. Feel comforted.

Monday : Sort out all music and newsletters for tomorrows rehearsal. Boy will this be well organised!!!!!!!!!!!!!!!! Ring round trying to find microphone leads used by powered by the son. Tim and Pauls phones engaged. Wonder optimistically if they are talking to each other to sort it out. Wonder whether to ring round to tell people we are meeting in the church tomorrow and not at Laura's. Decide to leave it to common sense and the Holy Spirit not necessarily in that order.

Tuesday : Elastic Band rehearsal day. Wait for long series of phone calls which usually interrupt my tea to ask if today is a rehearsal day. Receive phone call from Eleanor asking for list of songs that EB can actually play so Peter can plan the informal service at which we are to play. Feel that this is an excellent idea and put newsletter through vicarage door that night. Dont receive any more phone calls except one from Band member requesting return of video I had completely forgotten about. Try to put blame onto absent 12 string owning guitarist husband ransack lounge looking for video find acceptable substitute and leave for rehearsal. All members arrive except Russell who has other commitment. Two members seen out on the Green evangelising or eyeing up the local talent according to your point of view. Return to rehearsal with potential rehearsal watcher. Fishers of men here without a doubt! Put out all music in neat piles and request band members to select according to the list on the newsletter they have just been given. Twenty minutes later music all over floor total confusion. I scream and resolve NEVER to try to organise a band EVER AGAIN. Pray for peace calm grace and anything else I can think of. Collect in all music redistribute and start playing ten minutes later. Amazed to find that after sorting out vitriolic argument about who is to read out the prayer about God's love (!) that the prayer actually works. Spend about 30 second lost in wonder love and praise. Rest of rehearsal O.K.

Wednesday : My birthday. Await huge pile of cards arriving on mat from band members...
Go to work come back ransack house for huge pile of cards - Find one from sound man. Sue arrives with second card which is highly irreligious or possibly refers to playing the trombone. Not sure which Try to feel like religious trombone player - fail. Decide card is not to be explained to little ones! Receive letter from organisation saying that EB can now invest £100 in fair trading organisation. Previous limit £200. Good News! Eat birthday sweets and improvise on pitch pipe bought by sound man. Who says my playing is flat. Have ordered today four more EB T-shirts in Bristol must extract cash for same from appropriate band members.

Thursday : Receive request for reference for ex EB member. Not sure how vital ability to play slap bass is to working in service station. Look forward to eating cooked breakfast and being told to have a happy day by ex band member. Can think of a few days that would definitely not qualify when trying to sound check with said ex band member but decide to charitably overlook this and give good reference. Spend two hours trying to sort music into FOOLPROOF system. Daughter walks into lounge and stands on piles of music. Scream. Daughter moves quickly. Pray for protection for daughter if she EVER STEPS ON MUSIC AGAIN. Go to bed.

Friday : Arrive home looking forward to birthday meal. House empty. Family arrive from doctors with daughter with serious facial injuries after disagreement between daughter pony and trotting pole. Cancel meal. Watch drivel on T.V. with daughter whilst sympathising. Quiet uneventful evening after hectic E.B. type week. Thank God for family,band and take away meals.

Year Five

1997

January and February

All the Band members except one were in the village panto so we suspended rehearsals until the 19th February. We carried on having meetings at our house on the usual rehearsal night so that any band member who wanted to could still come. We used this time to find some interesting new gigs for the Band and in writing arrangements and harmonies for the songs we were using.

One of our gigs was set up in Thatcham at the request of the Methodist Minister who was in Aldbourne when we first began and had moved to Thatcham. We were thrilled to be asked to play at his church. The gig was called "Surfing the Sabbath" and took place in March

Another gig we were offered was the launch of a Christian book written by our vicar's wife. She was keen for us to play and demonstrate for children which was right up our street. We spent the rest of February practicing for both of these exciting events.

We were also accepted to play for the First Fruits Festival in Salisbury Cathedral which the Archbishop of Canterbury was attending. The only space for us was in the cloisters with no heat, light or power so we were back to playing entirely acoustically.

March

The practicing continued plus prayer for a band member and our cat Sullivan both of whom were ill. The band member recovered and the cat lasted another six years to the age of 23!

We had a complaint about tinsel on the church carpet which had fallen out of a violin case used at the Christingle Service. I tried to take this in my stride as I could think of a great many other things which could have fallen on the carpet but, thankfully, didn't!

I visited the Thatcham venue so that I knew what to expect. It was a lovely building and the Minister was very keen to see us, which was encouraging.

The book launch took place on the 8th March in the Church of England church in our village. The Band played action songs from 9am to 12 noon with only one break. One song "God made Noses" was a song I had written on the topic of disability. It proved very popular and a copy was requested by one of the people attending the book launch. Her daughter, who was with her, was partially sighted and they had really enjoyed doing the actions together.The copy was requested to enable Rainbow and Brownies to learn the song in the village where they lived.

The next day was the Mothers Day service and four of us from the Band taught one of the action songs to the congregation. The vicar asked for prayers for us for our forthcoming events, which was a very positive experience for us.

There was one more rehearsal before the Thatcham gig and one of the Band members was very nervous about how we would be received. I reminded myself that this was a young band needing much more reassurance than the other Band members who were now Powered by the Son. We were well received and organized an impromptu singing and dancing competition. My diary entry for the event reads;

"We surfed the Sabbath with a vengeance. It may take a while for the Sabbath to recover"

We were straight back into rehearsing for the First Fruits Festival at Salisbury Cathedral – the no heat, no light, no power gig. We had decided to focus on action songs for younger children as they seemed popular, were easy to play and were visually interesting. Between practices, we went to an Easter Egg Hunt in Aldbourne where a girl who had been at the Thatcham gig came up to me and said "Your Elastic Band is really good" We were thrilled at this unsolicited testimonial as it really boosted up our younger members.

At our next rehearsal, one of our Band members had rung up to ask if he could come despite having hit his finger with a hammer and couldn't play his instrument. Wrongly (as it turned out) I said yes. The Devil undoubtedly does find work for idle (and in this case injured) hands. My diary entry reads:

"X & Y tried to do something horrible to the grey cat using an elastic band but I think we stopped them"

The grey cat used to wander into the church quite frequently during our rehearsals.

I was concerned at this time, and rightly so, about the level of discipline I should exercise within the Band. My instinct is to work co-operatively and lead by example. However we had some boys who would have benefitted from stronger leadership I think. It's one of the areas (by no means the only one) where I don't think we got it quite right.

April

Chris and I took our children (our own, not the whole band!) to Spring Harvest which was a lovely break. Three of the older members (Now Powered by the Son) went to Spring Harvest as a group and came back with some great ideas including playing at Greenbelt or the Crossrhythms Festival.

After one more rehearsal it was the First Fruits Festival in Salisbury Cathedral. There were ten of us in all. We demonstrated one of our action songs for the Archbishop of Canterbury and had two Japanese tourists joining in with us as

their enthusiastic partners took photographs. I do wonder what was said about these pictures in Japan. After the gig we took the Band to Burger King and then a tea shop. These times were so important and enjoyable. Some of the feedback included:

> "Men in purple dresses (cassocks) all look alike to me"
> and
> "I never knew campanology was a swear word"

We had been placed in the cloisters next to some bell ringers and had to negotiate alternate slots of time for our playing.

Our next rehearsal was very constructive. I am certain that playing at Festivals helped the Band to progress more quickly. There were 11 of us in all, and we were starting to sound like the Elastic Band before Powered by the Son came into being, even though our line-up was so completely new.

We played for an informal service in the next village and managed to include a member of the congregation who we knew to be a good guitar player. It was a very uplifting service and we were able to find time to pray with one of our band members who had recently lost a close friend to cancer.

There were 13 attenders at our next rehearsal which was the last one before a Festival in Oxford organized by the Diocesan Children's Officer. She was the wife of our vicar and they were both very supportive of our work with the band.

May

Eleven of us went to Oxford for the Festival which was called a Gift Day. We led the worship and ran workshops teaching action songs. We had incorporated into our worship a sketch which involved two Band members pretending to be sheep. We asked the children at the Gift Day to let us know if they saw the sheep wandering off. This involved a lot of shouting and hilarity and led us into the song "I won't wander off" by Ishmael.

The music we used for worship included "Teach me to Dance", "I will Build my Church", "Come on and Celebrate" and "I am a New Creation" as well as a couple of songs I had written. We stayed all day and were very well received. It was a very positive experience for all the Band members.

The rest of May was taken up with very solid rehearsals. We had been invited back to Salisbury for another Festival and needed to make sure we knew what we would be doing. At least this time we had power and, as it was June and we were playing outside, the light and heat were not a problem.

The attendees were growing. There were 15 of us on the 7th May. We ran another Amen competition (as we had in the very early days)

June

This was an important month in a number of very different ways. One of the children in our village had died suddenly and unexpectedly of a heart problem. This completely overshadowed the Band rehearsal for two weeks and brought to the fore some painful memories. One of our members had had stillborn twin sisters who were in the graveyard of the church in which we were rehearsing. Also in the graveyard, was the grave of the child who had died that month. One of our Band members was going through personal struggles and another had been on a history trip to the Somme which had affected her deeply. We took time out from rehearsing for prayer and went into the graveyard to sing "Father God I wonder" beside the new grave. It was a very emotional experience. We found out later that someone in the village had heard our singing and found it very helpful.

The Salisbury Festival went well. We played both outside and inside and were blessed with good weather.

It was in June that we started to hold informal services which we ran as well as providing the music. They were held in our Methodist church and involved input from all the Band members. At the first there were 14 Band members in all as well as a good congregation. It was a lively service with quite a number of young children in the congregation.

Mark and Tim from Powered by the Son came as well. They had formed "Masterplan" with Mike (our first drummer) and had a slot to play at the Crossrhythms Festival which Chris, Paul and I were going to as well, so we discussed transport for this.

There were 16 at the next rehearsal and we planned an Elastic Band picnic for July. By this stage we were working hard at individual parts for different instruments, especially flute, and there was more prayer for people who had serious health problems and who were related to or known to Band members.

July

We started to plan a "Church Crawl" to raise money for Children in Need. The idea was to play in as many Anglican and Methodist church services in our area as possible on one Sunday morning, and ask for donations to Children in Need. This took a great deal of planning but we all felt enthusiastic about it.

We held our picnic and were blessed with wonderful weather. We played our gargling game with lemonade and Christian songs and even had a dog with us (a first for Elastic Band).

August

We managed a two week break in August as most Band members (including the leaders) were away, but we were back into rehearsals at the end of August for a Family Service in September in the Anglican church.

September

There was one more rehearsal before the Family Service. This was an 11 o'clock service and, therefore, the main service of the day. We were used to working in a more informal setting and so we worked hard on making sure we would fit in well to the more formal structure. We planned to play "More Love, More Power" (with prayers said over the music), "One shall tell another" (with a vine dance we were planning to teach), "I will build my church" (with actions) and "When the Spirit of the Lord" (with dancing). The church was full and included a baptismal party. The service went well, although I did feel under a certain amount of pressure because the sound we produced was very different from the normal worship music in the church. It was certainly very lively and we were able to encourage some dancing, which was great.

The rest of September was taken up with some very demanding rehearsals. At our maximum, we had 17 attending and I was struggling with how to fully engage all the members, especially the ones who were less able musically. One of the older Band members (though not an adult) suggested that good behaviour during rehearsals be made a condition of attending the bigger Festival events. That seemed a good idea to me and helped a lot. Also, Chris and Paul, as the male leaders spent time with the younger male Band members during rehearsals to help them to focus.

Sue and I were invited to the Diocesan Music Committee in Salisbury to talk about what we did (Not that we were entirely sure!). It was an eclectic mix and we were definitely at the far extreme but it was great to be asked.

October

This was when we started the Youth Alpha course with the Band. It was much needed, as, unlike our original members, these members had not made a commitment at the end of a mission at their school, nor had they attended a "Just Looking" course. The books were not well received by all of the members of the Band, although they were by most of them. Sue & I talked this through and split the session into two so that we did the Alpha material first. This worked much better.

However, we were still struggling with discipline for two or three of our members which was, understandably, concerning for the parents. In hindsight, we could have restricted the numbers but this would have cut across the Elastic concept. There were 4 adults to a maximum of 12 children which should have been manageable.

We decided (after a great deal of discussion and prayer) between the leaders to work one on one with the more "energetic" members and this worked well. We had also bought (with Band resources) some flags which were very popular. We were sometimes paid travelling expenses or, occasionally, a fee for the Festivals. We used this money to buy resources for the Band which are still used in our team churches. We spent a considerable amount of time on Youth Alpha and this really engaged the members, which was very encouraging.

Consent forms for events away from the village had been introduced by the Diocese and so these were prepared in readiness for the Church Crawl which we had started planning in July. The Crawl itself took place in November.

The end of October saw us organizing a Ghostbusters Party – a Christian alternative to Hallowe'en celebration. There were 11 of us and we played a variety of active Christian songs including a Christian variation of the Ghostbusters theme. We had some refreshments and an enthusiastic interactive group of partygoers.

November

This was an interesting month. There was still a lot of practice and admin to do for the Church Crawl. However, we also managed to fit in a 90 minute workshop at Theale, near Reading, on worship. There were three leaders and three of the older Band members in attendance which was the right number for this type of event, which we were leading. Afterwards, we went to MacDonalds.

Also, in November, one of our rehearsals was attended by 35 members of the Deanery Synod (not the Deanery Squad as Chris misinterpreted my writing!) The songs we played were "More Love, More Power", "Great is the Lord", "Teach me to Dance", "Praise Him on the Trumpet", "Lord I lift Your Name on High" and "We want to see Jesus lifted High"
Our playing was well received, and our percussionist really enjoyed the finger cymbals and fish-shaped tambourine we had bought, again from Band funds.

The Church Crawl came next and it was an amazing experience. The schedule was:

8 am Aldbourne St Michaels Church
9.30 Baydon C of E church
10.00 Ramsbury Methodists
10.30 Aldbourne Methodists
11.00 Aldbourne St Michaels church

The plan was to play one worship song in each service (either at the beginning or end) so as not to interrupt the flow of the service and to ask for donations to Children in Need. We had to play acoustically as there wasn't time to set up any amps or speakers. At the 10.30 Aldbourne Methodist service we were included as part of the sermon. We had let the local BBC Radio station know in advance what we were planning and they called us on our mobile phone (Not the driver!) between Baydon and Ramsbury. We were live on air – a first for the Elastic Band. This added to our enjoyment of a very special day. To have worshipped with so many different people both Methodist and Anglican was an experience of true fellowship.

Once we had banked the funds raised, we asked the Building Society to produce one of their large cheques seen at Children in Need and we went as a Band to the studios to present the cheque.

This was very enjoyable for the Band members and resulted in a very brief television appearance. Even the lady in the Building Society who wrote out the cheque was excited when she saw it on TV!

In November we ran our second Elastic Band Informal Service where we planned the service from start to finish. The title was "Act Your Shoe Size" and it was based on the theme of becoming as a child in order to enter the Kingdom. There were 16 Band members playing and singing. The service was based on Mark Chapter 10 verses 14 – 15. All the Band members brought along one of their baby shoes and the congregation worked out which shoe belonged to which Band member.

The service was encouraging and prayerful, particularly during the prayers when our keyboard player (who was 18) was playing and understood how to respond and lead. It was a humbling experience to acknowledge how far God had taken us.

We ended the month with a relaxing rehearsal playing some old favourites and getting our heads round some new ones for Christmas.

December

We took some time to work on Youth Alpha with the Band and then we were into rehearsals for a Methodist Family Service (which went well) and an ecumenical Christingle service (which didn't). We had rehearsed very thoroughly and we were well prepared. However, even half an hour before the service we were being asked to play songs we hadn't seen before. On reflection, this probably comes down to poor communication but it was a shame that such a wonderful service did not run smoothly.

Here is my Annual Report for 1997.

YES THERE DEFINITELY IS MORE THAN ONE KEY! READ SHOCK HORROR REPORT FOR ALL GUITARISTS ON PAGE FOUR

EB INTO THE FUTURE

December 25, 1997

1997

WE PLAYED AT MORE THAN 3 GIGS

WE LAUNCHED A BOOK

WE WORE REINDEER ANTLERS

WE TOLD PEOPLE OUR SHOE SIZE

WE MET SHAUN AND BARBARA

WE LOST SHAUN AND BARBARA

WE FOUND SHAUN AND BARBARA AGAIN

WE LOST SHAUN AND BARARA

WE MET SHAUN AND BARBARA AGAIN

ZZZZZZZZZZZZZZZZZZZZZZZZZZZZZZZZZZZZZZZZZZZZZZZZZZZZZZZZZZZZZZZZZZZZZZZZZZZZZZZZZZZZZZZZZZZZZZZZZZZZZ!

HAPPY NEW YEAR EVERYBODY

WHAT NEXT FOR EB?

Its going to be very hard to follow such an action packed year especially when Ros is already suffering from terminal exhaustion and an excess of tinsel.Her first New Years resolution is giong to be to stop improve her spelling. Her second Nwe Years resolution is to let you lot plan all the services because that seems like a really good idea! (She is going to have to work reaaly hard on that first resolution from the look of this) . But seriously (whatever that means!) we have a chance of helping to test run the module on Worship which has been put together by the good people of Salisbury and we are going to have a swimming party (or baptism in the Holy Spirit) so there is plenty to look forward to already. So keep praying and practising and we'll see you soon!

PRAYERS ANSWERED IN 1997 - HAMSTER RECOVERS FROM CONSTIPATION!!!!!!

Yes - you heard it here first. Those of you who are EB attenders know that during the latter part of 1997 we have embarked on an exciting and challenging and really amazing and impressive and -(look just get on with it will you this is really tedious) Do you want to have an argumnebt about this ? Fat chance you cant even spell argument! Oh yes I can its just the computer that cant! Well anyway for the one or two of you who are still reading we had this amazing..............prayer time every session and the most ama........and we got answers to lots of prayers. These included Ros getting a secretary, Laura 's parents getting planning permission,Anna's horse PONY getting well Hazel's father getting a job lots of people getting healed and most ama........ Nicholas' hamster was healed of constipation! What is so amazing about that I hear you ask? The point is on further investigation it turned out that the hamster actually had diarrhoea. Were there any prayers that were not answered I hear you ask. Well being mature Christians we know that all prayers are answered but sometimes the answer is NO.Thats why Ros' remote keyboard is still in the shop!

Fat Cat Gives Dog An Extra Biscuit!

CONTENTS	
GIG LIST	1
MEMBERS LIST	2
FOR SALE AND WANTED	3

YOUTH ALPHA COURSE INVADED BY AARDVAARKS

GIG REVIEW

So where were you on the 12th June 1997 and why weren't you moshing with the rest of civilisation at the Cross-rhythms Festival at Okehamptonin Devon? We were privileged to attend the Masterplan gig and see three people who are a lot taller than Sue and a fair bit taller than Ros entertaining the assembled crowds. I was impressed with the playing, the choice of material and the stage presence of the Band and it was a genuine pleasure to see them playing at a proper volume with a good sound system. The line up of Tim on bass, Mark on lead guitar and Mickey on drums worked well and although I dont know if the little boy Mark lifted on stage will need counselling for long he certainly wont forget the experience. The Festival spreads over three days and has some of the biggest CCM artists around (Yes as well as Masterplan!). It is well worth a visit if you like your music loud and non stop. (Incidentally there was a band in the all comers tent that purported to call themselves The Elastic Band but they werent a patch on you lot!)

ACT YOUR SHOE SIZE

This is the bit where I get to sound off about the last year. I have to say that my favourite bits where when we did get to act our shoe size and get into worship in a very relaxed way. The chance to put our own services together has been very much appreciated because the Elastic Band style does not always sit easily along side more traditional forms of worship especially in buildings with very difficult acoustics. Being invited by Jenny Hyson to work with children and adults in the Oxford Diocese has been very fulfilling. The church crawl was a great way to worship with lots of different people in a short space of time and the visit to the TV and Radio studio is something I wont forget. The video with the Band on is available as soon as I remember to pick it up from the shop. I do not yet know what 98 will bring but I do know God isnt finished with us yet!

YOUTH ALPHA FLUMMOXES THE ELASTIC BAND

Five months and 13 chapters and 49 pages and we have nearly reached the end of the Alpha course. Believe it or not all the members of the band have grasped the concept without much questioning. Initially food was the thing they wanted and they have probably been sadly disappointed until the baptism in the Holy Spirit at Marlborough Leisure Centre where food was abundant. We have gone from concurrent prayers to debates on crocodiles and we all know Hazel is a banana (oops that is a quiz answer). You may have guessed that we get sidetracked easily but at least it isnt boring. To come we have "How can I make the most of the rest of my life" WOW

Well here is the shock horror report mentioned on the first page. Us pianists do realise that sometimes guitarists do struggle with some of the more advanced concepts in the musical sphere like diminished 7ths and suspended 4ths (and we are not just talking about Pete and Tim here). As a result we have developed an amazing new mnemonic just for you. Are you ready? Fat Cat Gives Dog An Extra Biscuit! You now have all the information you need to work out all the sharps in whatever key and how many there are likely to be. If you look on page one you will even find a cartoon to go with it! Generous or what!

MEN IN PURPLE DRESSES ALL LOOK ALIKE -
LUDLOW 2 CHAPTER 67 VERSE 17

GIG LIST 1997 - HOW - WHY - WHERE -

8th March - Launch of Jenny Hyson' Book in St Michaels

15th March - Surfing the Sabbath Soul Party

12th April - First Fruits Festival in Salisbury Cathedral (No light No heat No power!)

20th April - Come and Join The Dance - St Nicholas Church Baydon

3rd May - Gifft Day - Oxford

14th June - Salisbury Diocesan Children's Festival - Salisbury Cathedral

22nd June - No Audition - Aldbourne Methodist Chapel - Informal Service

7th September - Family Service - St Michaels Aldbourne

31st October - Ghostbusting - Aldbourne Youth Club

8th November - Feed My Sheep - Thatcham - Oxford Diocese Workshops

16th November - Children In Need - Church Crawl - St Michaels - St Nicholas - Ramsbury Methodists - Aldbourne Methodists - Childrens Party Baydon School - St Michaels Aldbourne

EVEN MORE GIGS

23rd November - Act Your Shoe Size - Aldbourne Methodist Chapel Informal Service

21st December - Christmas Family Service - Aldbourne Methodist Chapel

24th December - Christingle Service - St Michaels Aldbourne

Puzzle: Why are these Alice's friends?

MEMBERSHIP LIST - THE WHOS AND THE WHATS

- Ros and Nicola
- Sue and Hannah
- Paul
- Chris # 2
- Nicholas # 2
- Laura
- Matthew
- Elly
- Tabitha
- Anna
- Hazel
- Pete
- Becky
- Russell
- Alex # 2-
- Lizzie
- Kathryn
- Grey Cat
- Bat
- Shaun
- Barbara
- Brian
- Lucy
- Emily Rose
- **It could be you!**
- These people and things are listed in order of pharosidity

Dateline 1997
Scurvey came in with a report of a mysterious occurrence in a remote country church. The circumstances were weird enough for me to open a + file.
Aldbourne Wiltshire
We arrived on a cold and misty night. There was lots of blue light around but the re again there always seems to be wherever we go. There was an unearthly sound coming from a church. We asked a passing villager what was in there. But he only rolled his eyes and ran away shrieking "Its Tuesday - Its Tuesday". We walked towards the church between tombstones leaning at crazy angles. The tomb stones didn't look too good either.

The weird sounds were getting louder. Scurvey drew her gun and leaned against the door jamb. The jam ran down her coat glistening like unearthly blood. I pushed on the door which opened with a loud

7

YOU SAW IT HERE FIRST - THE ONE AND ONLY EB QUIZ - HOW AWAKE WERE YOU DURING 97?

THE EB QUIZ

After the stunning success of last years quiz we have decided to have another one. That way we know who stays awake during the year. So a valuable prize to the first person or animal to get this lot right!

- What was the name of Jenny Hyson's new book
- Who sneezed at the Methodists Christmas service
- How many churches did we visit during the Church Crawl
- How many people saw us on TV
- How much did we raise for Children In Need
- Who described Jesus as a sin magnet and why
- Who is the ultimate Ghostbuster
- Who had the prettiest shoes at the Informal service
- What grade did Sue pass in her gymnastics examinations
- How many channels does Paul have on his new desk and how proud is he of it
- What have crocodiles got to do with youth alpha
- Who suggested we could be on the Antiques Roadshow and why

FOR SALE AND WANTED

Wanted : Shoulders to cry on and more sleep
Apply to Ros and Sue

For Sale: Transposition for I Wont Wander Off
Ideal for any instrument other than an e flat saxophone
Apply to Ros

Wanted : Even more gadgets
Apply to Chris

Wanted : Identification badges for men in purple dresses
Apply to Pete Ludlow

Wanted : Ear mufflers for people who stand next to campanologists
Apply to Paul Newman

Wanted : Pyramid scaffolding
Apply to Elly Anna and Alex

Wanted : Script for TV appearance
Apply to Alex

Wanted : Prayer support
Apply to Any Band Member

QUIZ CONTINUED

- What fruit is Hazel most like
- Who scared who when he shouted at him from the roof of St Michaels
- Whose grave did we play beside and what did we play
- Who won Band member of the week and why
- Which charity has adopted God Made Noses as its song and why
- Where have we been this year for our post gig relaxations and why did we send them some money
- How did we find out that Japanese people love action songs
- What did Hazel say to the child who asked her if she was a real sheep

creak and as I did so the noise grew louder. Then I saw them. My blood ran cold. The heating wasn't on. The noise was infiltrating my brain. Wierd shapes danced in front of my eyes. Loud screams rent the air. As Mouldy raised his head he could see them charging towards him. That noise.........That noise..............

Will Scurvey ever get that jam off her coat?.......

Will Mouldy ever snog Scurvey?......

Out there the truth is....

Is there out the truth....

The truth is out there.. no..

The truth is in here!

To be continued - every Tuesday at 7.30pm - come and find out more.

Year Six

1998

January

By the 6th January we were keen to get going and see what 1998 had to offer. Although it was the Band's final year, it was a good time for us all and we were able to enjoy putting into practice what we had learned since 1993.

We combined Youth Alpha work with practicing for a service we were organizing at the Methodists and we had a Pool Party. We hired the local swimming pool, recorded tapes of Christian music and had lots of fun.

The people running the pool enjoyed our music and were very interested in what we were doing. We enjoyed a party buffet afterwards and didn't make too much mess. It was a great way to start the year.

The Methodist service on the 25th January was one we had put together as a band. We were conscious that we used, in the main, music written within the last 20 years. We wanted to encourage the congregation (some of whom were elderly) to think about welcoming the new songs as well as enjoying the old. Sue and I wanted the Band members to think about this as well. So….we took this as our theme for the service and brought with us (for the purposes of comparison)

(a) An electronic metronome and an old-fashioned metronome made of wood and metal
(b) A dust pan and brush and a vacuum cleaner
(c) An old and a young hamster belonging to one of the Band members

Looking back, as I can now, I feel this was what we did best. Everyone in the congregation was engaged (especially when the hamsters got out of the cages!). The message (that each had a great deal to offer) was clearly communicated and we all had fun doing it. Here is the service plan.

OUT WITH THE OLD IN WITH THE NEW
SERVICE PLAN

At the start R will be playing traditional music on the Chapel Organ to be selected by him

A:Welcome to the service explain the title and introduce the reading
B: First reading Colossians Ch 3 Verses 2-3

ALL: First song I am a new creation

A: Explain that the reading talked about getting rid of the old self but do we always want to get rid of old things automatically?

A and R compare old and new metronomes N talks about his hamster and his sisters hamster and explains why he likes the old hamster

R suggests looking further into the reading to find out more

B: Second reading Colossians Ch 3 Verses 8-10

S talks about old and new coca cola and then old and new wine

ALL: Second song One shall tell another

R points out that we are going to need healing and forgiveness if we are going to leave all the anger behind so suggests we hear more from the reading

M: Third reading Colossians Ch 3 Verse 11

R introduces the re writing of Jew or Gentile and then this is sung as re written A E and T write out the negative emotions that come out e.g. pride anger etc

ALL: Third song Jew or Gentile and S points out we are going to need God's help if the re writing of the last song was anything to go by

L: Fourth reading Colossians Ch 3 verses 14-15 during the reading R starts to play Make me a channel of your peace very quietly. As the reading finishes R introduces the song and asks God in prayer to show us how to leave our sinful selves behind and become channels of God's peace! It will be sung with an instrumental verse between the second and third chorus and then we will sing it ot the end. At the end R will carry on playing and A T and E will cut up the pieces of paper with the negative emotions on

If there is time S will demonstrate the dustpan and brush as against the vacuum cleaner using the bits of paper from the cutting up exercise. If not R will introduce O for a thousand tongues to sing starting with L singing the first verse as a solo

ALL: The Grace
END

February

February was a relaxing month. We didn't have anything major coming up so we had time to enjoy doing some different things. This included a pop quiz and a film quiz made up by different band members. We talked about whether the band wanted to play at the school they attended. The band members decided against this but they were keen to play in our local village churches both Methodist and Anglican. We explored the use of deaf signing. We first used this when we played The Gift and it proved very popular. It added a new dimension to the songs and was a good tool for communicating with everyone – whether they had hearing issues or not. I was once taken to task by the parents of a child with serious hearing problems. I had been teaching the actions to a well known Ishmael song during a service. The actions were not deaf signs and had left their daughter feeling very confused. It is a lesson worth remembering. We finished the month by starting to practice for the Christian Aid service which we always enjoyed.

March 1998

We decided to learn some African songs for the Christian Aid service. They were not very easy and involved four part harmony so they stretched us to our limit (and a bit beyond!). we worked out how to sign the African songs and listened to some Matt Redman songs. We met at the house of one of the band members when it was very cold. Our usual meeting place now was the Anglican church but it was very cold in the middle of winter.

April 1998

We had some very lively sessions (which helped to keep us warm) doing the African songs and some Ishmael songs with deaf signs. We also fitted in another pop quiz and a check list of attitudes to the Bible which Sue had found. Unsurprisingly we found that the most popular bits of the Bible were the gory bits!

May 1998

At this time we had 11 regular attenders in addition to the adults. We carried on practising for the Christian Aid Service and we were asked to play 10 traditional hymns for the Fete Service which is held in June every year on the village green. It was a sign of the village's confidence in us that they wanted us there and they wanted traditional hymns on modern instruments – a good example of the best of the old and the best of the new.

The Christian Aid Big Breakfast and Service took place on the 10th May and was very well received (especially the bacon!). We were thrilled to welcome back Sally who had attended our first ever session (1st June 1993). Her skills as a flautist had grown and so we were able to add some interesting flute parts for the Fete Service.

June 1998

Practising for the Fete Service was very interesting as some of the traditional hymns were completely new to the band members. I worked out some very simple clarinet parts which worked well with the hymns.

To our great excitement a lay reader in our team had been short listed for the preacher of the year competition. We talked about this and the entire Band signed a card sending her our best wishes and congratulations. She had always been very supportive of the Band. Our last practice before the Fete Service was in the church as we needed to have all the drum kit in place. The rehearsal clashed with the Scotland v Morocco match (23.6.1998) and so the Walkmans appeared again. Nevertheless we managed to have a good rehearsal. The Fete Service was beautiful especially as we were outside and blessed with sunshine. We had brought our flags with us so it was a colourful service.

July 1998

By now we knew that Sue was going to leave the village because of her husband's job. We reached a decision that as there was no one else to take Sue's place, it was time to bring the Band to an end. This was a great sadness for all of us but also a time to reflect and learn from all that we had experienced.

We were invited to play for our last service in November at Broadchalke near Salisbury. There was a great deal of planning to do. The Bishop of Salisbury was coming to Broadchalke for a service to celebrate an important anniversary and the service was to include a blessing for those couples who had been married in the church. The service was to be quite long and formal. Therefore, very sensibly, the organisers asked us to arrange a party for the children of the parents who would be attending the service. We were given a free hand with the planning which was very helpful. We used action songs, wrote a sketch about the hired hand who abandoned the sheep, a game involving chocolate and we pretended to be a train. There were 40 attendees all under 12 who had a great time and joined in well. The only problem we had was that we had arranged to be there at 9 am for a 10.45 start. The caretaker came to let us in at 10.10! Apparently they had been expecting two people and a guitar. The Bishop of Salisbury joined us once the service in the main service was over in the church.

After we had packed up we went to Burgerking in Salisbury for our final de-brief. We always enjoyed relaxing together after all the hard work. It was sad to think we had come to the end of this particular journey but we were excited about all we had enjoyed and learnt along the way.

Carnival, Aldbourne

Children in Need

Southwick Party

“Alive”, Salisbury

Powered by the Son

Part 2:

The "How to" part: Advice and pointers

HOW TO REHEARSE AND HOW NOT TO REHEARSE

Band members will probably come to every band meeting expecting to play some music and so that has to be part of every meeting. However, there is a huge difference between running a Worship Group and a Band. I have been involved with both and enjoy both but for the young people my view is that the Band has much more to offer.

The main difference is that the focus of each meeting must be on developing your relationship with the young people. What you do about that will vary but for at least the first eight to ten meetings my view is that you should not have any particular event in mind to play for. This is because if you have, the focus becomes the music and not the relationships. In that respect we were lucky with the start of the Elastic Band as no-one knew we existed at first and so we were not asked to play for anything for the first few weeks. Looking back on it this was a good thing as it made Susie and I work harder at thinking of other things to do.

Here are some examples of what we did and why (although sometimes the reason was just that it seemed like fun!).

1. Play the gargling game. Each band member has to gargle with lemonade (not easy) and gargle a tune that the others have to guess. If you have a group that is used to going to church you can restrict this to Christian songs but you might have to be a bit flexible. You need to cover the floor with plastic as the lemonade goes everywhere and don't play it in a car as it gets on the seats (and the roof I seem to remember!)

2. Have a competition for the best setting of Amen that any band member can come up with and ask an adult member of the congregation to come along to judge this. Pick someone fairly tolerant who knows how to handle situations like this sensitively and it cant be a parent of any of the band members.

3. Have a competition for a rap based on anything vaguely Christian. Our rap had to be based on Christmas and I seem to remember that donkeys featured heavily.

4. Have quizzes based on music and the Bible e.g. how many musicians did David have? This will put any moans about the band being too loud into perspective. There may be someone in your church who will be willing to set the questions for you and remember that the more you involve other church members the more they will understand how hard you are working and the more they are likely to pray for you.

5. Ask local Christian adult musicians to come along to the Band to demonstrate their skills and talk to the band members. This was really popular. On three separate occasions we had a lead guitarist, a bass guitarist and a drummer who brought his entire kit and more along and spent a long time talking to us and letting the band members loose on various bits of percussion. It was a memorable evening.

6. Go out and eat food.

7. Encourage the band members to say a short prayer at the beginning and end of each session. Its best to model this at first and keep the prayers really short – Thank you God for music Amen is a good start.

8. If you haven't had something such as a Just Looking course to set the Band off you might like to think about running a youth Alpha alongside the Band or some other suitable short course. We did this and found it interesting when we had an influx of young people who had been too young to attend the mission that started the Band off at the beginning. We learnt a lot about each other and did a fair bit of colouring in. We used the first half hour of the rehearsal for the Alpha course and the second half for playing.

9. Keep the rehearsals reasonably short. We tried to stick to an hour as usually we had had enough by then. When the Band got too big (we had about 18 members at one stage) we split this into two groups roughly by age and had two consecutive one hour rehearsals. Remember that your band members will have lots of school work and possibly other activities to think about and fit in.

10. As the actual rehearsal time is fairly short be organised at the beginning and the end. I tended to be the Martha in this situation and rushed around putting up music stands, getting the music out and generally behaving as if I was the only one who did any work and Susie was good at chatting to the band members as they arrived and finding out what was going on for them. I think its better to involve the Band members in getting used to setting up for themselves but somehow that always seemed like too much hard work. If you find that no-one wants to set out the stands and music and everyone just want to talk to the band members you probably have a discussion group and not a band. If you still want a band see if anyone who is a musician will help

on the practical front but leave you to talk. Just make sure that they can cope with a certain level of chaos.

CHOOSING THE BEST MUSIC

This is one of the most important things to get right when you are running the Band. We got it right sometimes and wrong sometimes and here is what we learnt.

1. Always pick the best example of the music that you are playing. Don't use weak tunes or weak words. If you aren't sure about either of these enlist the help of someone whose opinion you respect in the church. This is one of the ways that you can reach out to other people in the church to build up relationships and confidence in your work.

2. Don't limit yourself to one type of music or music from one era. I used everything from O For A Thousand Tongues through to Ishmael songs such as The Mustardseed song . Variety is the key. Another very important point here is that it is easy to be dismissive of old songs or just songs that you personally don't like. This gives out a poor message to young people. There is nothing wrong with disliking a specific song for a specific reason. I have never liked any song that portrays Jesus as meek and mild because I don't believe he was but it is wrong to say all old hymns are bad. They aren't and respect is something that young people can understand and learn from. We have included a list of all the songs and hymns we used in the Diary section just to give you ideas and for no other reason. If you never use any of them that's fine but if you are having a very bad day and can't think of any at all the list might just give you one less thing to have to think about!

3. Use songs and hymns creatively so that you are modelling good worship leading to the Band. I always remember one occasion when we used More Love More Power as an accompaniment to prayer (it works really well if the prayers are said over the music on the second or third time through). The young people wrote the prayers and the feeling of power that this generated was almost tangible. Songs are for much more than singing.

4. Always play songs that the Band is capable of playing at the time. Because of the elastic nature of the Band the line up and experience of its members changed a lot and sometimes we were doing well if we managed Come on and Celebrate at other times we could play Did You Feel the Mountains Tremble and sound convincing. However, I was always happy to go back to the simple stuff if I felt that the musicians were struggling. I am sure we have all had less than good worship experiences where musicians of whatever age were struggling to cope musically. This is not honouring to God. We owe it to God to consistently work to improve what skills He has given us (whatever they may be) and God deserves our very best. This does not mean that until we are note perfect we cannot play in worship situations but the musicians do have a duty to the congregation to enhance the worship and not detract from it. This can be a dilemma when working with young people in the elastic way that we did. I will always remember one occasion when our local Methodist minister who had heard us in our very early days asked very politely if we would ever get any better. Susie (who was always very honest and direct) said no on the basis that that was not what we were about. In fact we did improve as the Band members

practised and gained experience but also we got better at choosing suitable material and using it wisely.

5. Insist (and I mean INSIST) on being involved from the very beginning in choosing the music for any service that the Band is asked to play for. This will enable you to keep to paragraph 4. I am sure we will all have had the experience of being asked to play something at the last minute. My favourite example of this was when I was asked to play a completely new hymn I had never seen before actually during the Service! As sight reading is one of my strong points and I did not have the band with me that day it was not a problem but young people need time to rehearse and practice properly. Ideally I always liked to know the songs four weeks in advance (and yes I do know how unrealistic that might be!). The other way around this is to give the person leading the service a list of what the band can actually play and ask them to choose from it. I have used this method successfully but you do need to be firm sometimes.

6. Always think about who is likely to attend the service and think about the music they are used to hearing (if any). My experience is that because you are working with young people congregations on the whole are sympathetic which is helpful. However, this must not be abused and if you are asked to play for a main festival service (such as Harvest Festival or Christmas) don't expect people to thank you if you ditch all the golden oldies in favour of the latest Matt Redman that you love but no-one else has even heard of. You will make the life of your Minister unbearable and might never be asked again. Yes I have made this mistake and yes I have learned from it. It does not mean that you only ever play exactly what the congregation wants

as there may be a need to grow in a new direction but this is not your decision alone. This is a good time to remind you that music ministry is a servant ministry and you will be reminded of this again and again (every time you get something wrong!).

HOME AND AWAY

However unlikely it seems there will come a point when you feel capable of playing for some type of service or event. At first the thought terrified me but young people do need a focus for what they are involved in and once I realised that we had something to offer and people are usually very understanding I became more and more ambitious for the Band. As a matter of interest when I asked some old band members to let me know for the purposes of this book what they had enjoyed most about the band, playing for other people was the choice for two out of the first three that I asked. In particular one of the Band members said that playing for people she didn't know had built up her confidence and helped her when she started doing competitive dressage with her horse! It does show that we have no idea how much we can help other people until we try.

I have called this section home and away because you need to think about both. It is sensible to start playing for services in your own church where the facilities are known to you and the young people will feel at home. Hopefully you can be guaranteed some sympathetic congregation members if only because they are related to the band members. Some type of informal service is the best way to begin with. You need to tell the service organiser exactly what the band can cope with. Do not underestimate how important the service will be to the band even if they have attended the same service as worshippers many times. Being at the front and in a band is completely different and will feel very special to them. Here are the basics that you need to be careful about if you and the band are to have a good experience and not too much explaining to do to the people in charge!

1. Make sure you have at least four weeks notice of what you will be playing and if possible the order you will be playing it in. You will get better at doing things at short notice but one band member put as a pet hate having to transpose music 10 seconds before playing it. That is not something to attempt until you have played together for a long time.

2. Make sure everyone in the band knows who is playing the introduction and how you are going to start the song or hymn. Usually its easier to have a keyboard only introduction at first until you are all confident.

3. Make sure everyone knows exactly how the piece will end and how many repetitions there are to be. There are times when you will want to be led by the spirit but this is not one of them. That may seem spiritually unsatisfying but the most important thing is for your young band members to feel confident and that takes time and trust. We did reach a point where we knew each other well enough to follow if one band member felt called to carry on playing and lead us in some informal worship but that takes time.

4. Try to have all the music for each band member in the right order so that all they have to do to find the next piece is turn over. I have spent many happy and not so happy hours on my lounge floor on a Sunday afternoon putting music into order for a Sunday evening service. If this happens draw on as much help as you can get so you are not alone.

5. Start setting things up at least an hour before the service actually begins. Sometimes I allowed longer depending on how many violins I might have to tune and how

many stands I had to put up. The more time you have the less stressed you will be and the better things will run. I always remember turning up two hours before a service to start setting up only to find that the building was not open and it took us an hour to locate someone with a key. When they saw how much equipment we had (this was five years into the band) they realised why this created a problem for us and said that they were only expecting a couple of guitars! If you have any extra time at the beginning (and usually you wont) you can always use it for extra prayer so its never wasted.

6. Leave yourself enough time at the end to clear up properly and sort the music out. Remember that it will have been sorted through and probably thrown on the floor at some point by each band member and you don't want to be the one chasing after it weeks later when it is under a pew at the back of the church. Tidying up is important because this is part of your reputation which is crucial. It doesn't matter if the band can play

beautifully if they leave a mess behind and behave in a way which is disrespectful or unhelpful to other people in the church. This is a servant ministry and the time to start modelling this is now.

7. Its fine and in fact crucial to have a laugh and a good time but never at someone else's expense. When we were playing at a Cathedral Festival we had to stop our sound check for Evensong which was a real pain for us as we wanted to sound our best but that is exactly what we did. We then had to resolve the difficult spiritual issue of whether it was ok to play Frisbee in the Cathedral while Evensong was continuing and came up with the solution that it was ok as long as you didn't let the Frisbee hit the floor and so make a noise! Ok so we didn't find that in Colossians but at least it made some kind of sense.

8. Always try to have a group prayer at the start of the service. The best ones we had were where we could put our arms around each other and just have a group hug. Sometimes some of the band members will be nervous and you need to help them. Sometimes you will feel nervous and they can help you. All of this only works if it's God's will anyway and asking for His help is the most important thing of all.

9. Have a word however short with all the band members after the service. They will want to tell you all sorts of things right the way from – I didn't find any of the music and didn't play anything which needs a "never mind" answer to wow that was amazing – I didn't realise how much fun it would be. If there isn't a chance to do that, ask the band members at the next band meeting how it was for them. This is incredibly important because you will learn a great deal about

where they are spiritually as well as just caring about what kind of an experience it was for them.

All of these points will become automatic and some of them may be too obvious to even write down but I got it wrong as often as I got it right at the beginning so I think it is helpful to have this just as a checklist.

When you are playing away the list gets longer! This is because there are more variable factors to take into account. So here goes

1. All the points that I have set out for playing at home still apply but you might need to get there even earlier if there are sound checks to do. Its far better not to see this as a hassle but to treat it as a trip out that you can enjoy. If you don't find being with young people enjoyable you might need to look at whether this is what you want to be doing at all. When we had to be there for a sound check at 4 pm before an overnight festival we got there in the early afternoon so we could have time to eat and chat about what was happening and life in general. I still remember it as a really special time.

2. If at all possible visit the venue before you go to play there. You need to find out where your power, light and heat will be, what the acoustics are like and what the atmosphere of the building is. These things can make all the difference to what you play if you have any choice. If you cant visit then talk in detail to the organisers and remember that they might not know what you need to know if they aren't musicians who play in bands. Sometimes its really simple because there aren't any facilities at all and then its acoustic or nothing! That's fine as long as you know in advance

when you are planning what to do. One festival we played for where the Archbishop of Canterbury was in attendance was memorable because when I started asking my usual list of questions I was told very firmly that the answers were simple. There was no heat, no light and no power! I just hope that referred to the venue and not the Holy Spirit! As it turned out we had an excellent time and at least one group of Japanese tourists left the Festival with some very odd photos when they joined in with us for the action songs.

3. Its good to have a strong group identity when you are away from home. This is helpful for you, for the organisers, for the people there who are wondering who on earth you are, and anyway its good fun. We dealt with this by having customised airbrushed T-shirts designed for us. That sounds very flash and expensive but it wasn't as they were only about £15 each and looked amazing. Every band member who wanted one could have their own instrument on the T-shirt plus the Elastic Band man. You will see them on the photos throughout the book. We also had a banner made for us by a member of our church congregation which added to our identity and covered up some of the wires when

we were using keyboards and electric guitars. The visuals are important and they are something that some members of the band will find very interesting and important for them.

4. There are more practicalities to deal with when you are playing away. You have to have consent forms signed by a parent or guardian for every band member under 18 and you need to check that your insurance covers you properly. Check this out with your church leaders and if necessary your insurers. We never had to make a claim but its very important to check these things out as you want to take the best possible care of the band. Make sure you know exactly where you are going and who is taking who. Sometimes it will be possible to claim travel expenses if you keep a proper record of your mileage and clear this with the organisers beforehand. Make sure everyone comes back at the end especially after an overnight stay. We did think we had lost a band member once when he went home with a different person from the one he travelled with. We wondered if he was asleep

under a pew somewhere but he was tucked up in bed after being up all night at the Festival.

5. Take photos and videos wherever possible. Its great to watch them together afterwards and let everyone talk about their experiences. In years to come when you are too old and frail to carry amplifiers you can look at them and remember the "good" times!

6. Try to develop some kind of ritual around the away days. We had a ritual of going to Burgerking afterwards for a de-brief and although we didn't always manage it we usually found somewhere to chill afterwards. We had long discussions about all sorts of things including completely irrelevant things but had a really good time as a group and we could check out if anyone had really struggled with anything while we were away.

7. If possible try to have an event where you link up with another church and if possible stay overnight with the members of the other church. This really can be life changing stuff for all sorts of reasons and can really benefit both your group and the other church in all sorts of ways. We only managed this once but have some incredibly special memories from that time. The other church was only about 40 miles away but it felt much further and was from a different denomination which added to the interest. I tried to arrange an event with a church in Jersey but never quite got there with the idea. Still its something to think about.

ACOUSTIC OR ELECTRIC?

I realise that this title might not mean anything to some people but it is as well to read it as it could affect how your band develops in the long run. For others the answer to this question might be obvious in which case you probably don't need to read it at all.

The point I am making in the title is that there are different sorts of instruments that can be played in different ways in different settings and you need to work out which is best for you. When instruments are played acoustically it means that there is no electronic or artificial amplification of the sound which has its good and bad points. When we started we were entirely acoustic. By the time we finished we were almost entirely electric and so we had lots of experiences of the advantages and disadvantages of each approach. To save you making all our mistakes (and this is the area where we made the most) here is what we found out.

ST. JOHNS

THE ADVANTAGES OF THE ACOUSTIC APPROACH

1. SPEED – It is a lot quicker to start playing at the beginning of a session or service if you do not have to worry about amplification at all. You simply get the instruments out, tune them if you need to and then play. It's as easy as that. If it's hard to hear, say, the flutes then put them nearer the front and put the loud guitarist at the back or even outside (yes we have done that!). At the end you just pack up the instruments and walk away. It might sound trivial to talk about speed as the first consideration but at our most complex it took us three hours to setup and pack away and that is a lot of your precious time. I must admit that my absolute preference is to play acoustically but there are reasons why its not always the right thing to do

2. KIT – You need a lot less kit to play acoustically and so this saves money and complexity. All electric kit costs money and needs fixing when it breaks which it does a lot if you move around with it. So that's one more reason for the acoustic approach

3. FEAR – The acoustic approach looks less scary to people who are only used to hearing an organ. They can usually cope with flutes, violins, acoustic guitars and various brass instruments. They start looking worried (and on one famous occasion – terrified) when the drum kit and the electric guitars appear. We all know that perfect love overcomes fear but they might find that perfectly loving your adorable teenage boys with the drumsticks does not come easily. It's definitely worth working on but as with so many things there is a lot to be said for tact and starting acoustically might be the best solution.

Q: What's black and white and makes a lot of noise?
A: A Zebra with a set of drums

4. PERSONNEL – You need fewer people to run the sound side of things if you are playing acoustically. You don't need a sound engineer or someone to tell you the balance is all wrong (who is likely to be someone who just appears when kit appears but has no qualifications whatsoever as a sound engineer). You don't need someone to carry all the incredibly heavy amplifiers and mixers etc etc and you don't need all the people in the music shop who want to sell you all the said amplifiers etc. It's a much easier ride

5. ABILITY – playing acoustically means that what you play is what they hear in its pure unvarnished form. Having spent some time in different bands I know how much can be changed and masked with electronic devices. Believe me, I now know why so many live bands sound so different from their studio produced CDs. Therefore, if you play acoustically you have to practise and learn to play as skillfully as possible and I do firmly believe that that is what God expects from us and is entitled to. During my teenage years my interest

in my faith was coloured by my image of two out of tune guitars and a tambourine at the front of a half empty building. I know how wrong that was and how superficial I was but we do have a duty to do everything we reasonably can to encourage rather than discourage others and our skills have to be developed.

6. BUILDINGS – It may be that you will spend time playing in stone buildings without any carpet or curtains. It can be very challenging to say the least to find the right sound when it is being produced electrically. The acoustic sound is a gentler one which might reverberate less harshly. My knowledge of sound engineering is very limited but that is just my experience.

So – it look as if acoustic is the way to go? But its not all good news so here is the down side.

THE DISADVANTAGES OF THE ACOUSTIC APPROACH

1. To some teenagers – and at one time I was one of them – acoustic looks boring. It can also sound boring if its unadventurous. It has a serious image problem. Whilst I know that we are talking about worship and not image this is relevant to working with young people. If the only way to get teenagers into your church is to invite their electric guitars and drum kits in and see if they follow are you prepared to do that? Your answer may be different from mine and none the worse for that but at least think about it. I would rather have twenty electric guitars with their owners than an empty church.

2. At some big events even acoustic instruments will need some form of amplification. You then get into a debate

about how to amplify a flute and which guitar to take with you. Before you know it you are into the whole amplification debate anyway and the more you know about it the better worship musician you will be.

3. Electric instruments can do more than acoustic ones. I deliberately did not say more interesting things as opinions vary on that one. However, there is no doubt that you can make sounds with synthesizers (Ice Rain being one of my favourites) that do not exist in the acoustic world. Therefore, you are enhancing the worship opportunities you can offer to congregations. This does bring with it a responsibility to use the equipment wisely and not try to use every single sound in your flash new keyboard just because you want to. I doubt very much if the use of Saw Wave does much for Servant King or I'm Special.

4. All the problems listed in the first list have an upside. For example because electric equipment needs more people your opportunities for evangelism rocket without any great effort on your part. I didn't realise how true this was until I found that the young men in the music shop I use a lot each had their own experience of playing in worship and were happy to talk about it. I got a far more positive response when I went in and was genuinely surprised at the interest they took in helping me build up my collection of fruit based percussion for the Sunday School.

5. Because sound equipment can mask sound it can also help if you have inexperienced musicians who really want to get involved. OK so perhaps they cant play a violin like an angel but they may be able to hold down a chord on a keyboard which can be synthesized to sound like a much fuller sound. Also if all your sound

is going through one sound desk you can choose which instruments to quieten down if a serious problem is apparent. However, use this carefully. Young people

are just young and not stupid. They will know if you are consistently taking out all their sound and will tell you. Having said that I was once playing at an Alpha event when I failed to realise that as the song changed key I had changed my synthesizer key but not my on board monitor key. I knew it sounded awful but had no idea why. The sound man just took me out until I had sorted myself out and I was eternally grateful. It can happen to anyone.

6. Although generally speaking acoustic kit is cheaper we all know that a Stradivarius costs a lot more than a Les Paul guitar so there is a balance in there and in my experience if someone is really keen to play an instrument they will raise the money somehow. I do realise that I live in an affluent area and perhaps that wont always be the case. If the cost of instruments is a

real difficulty then I do feel this something that the church should look at as part of its funding for work with young people. I suspect that there are also ways of obtaining grants for this type of problem but I have not investigated. We did find that once we were playing at Festivals we were able to raise some of our own funds and used these to buy some percussion instruments and flags as well as investing in a Fair Trade organisation we heard about at a service we played for. This could have been used to fund the purchase of specific instruments if need be.

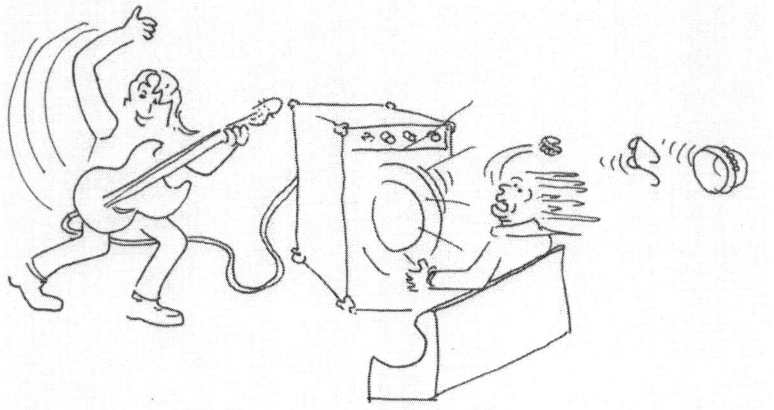

7. Careful sound engineering can help with the problem of buildings that are not user friendly. I don't know as much about this subject as I probably should but I do know that there are ways in which the sound engineer can help rather than hinder.

So all in all the way you go is up to you or rather up to your young people. We started off completely acoustic and that felt completely right at the time. As the young people got older we transferred across to a more electric approach and at one time ran two bands - one of each. There are times and places for both of them and don't forget that if you are offered a "no heat no light no power gig" you will need to have your recorder skills up to scratch!

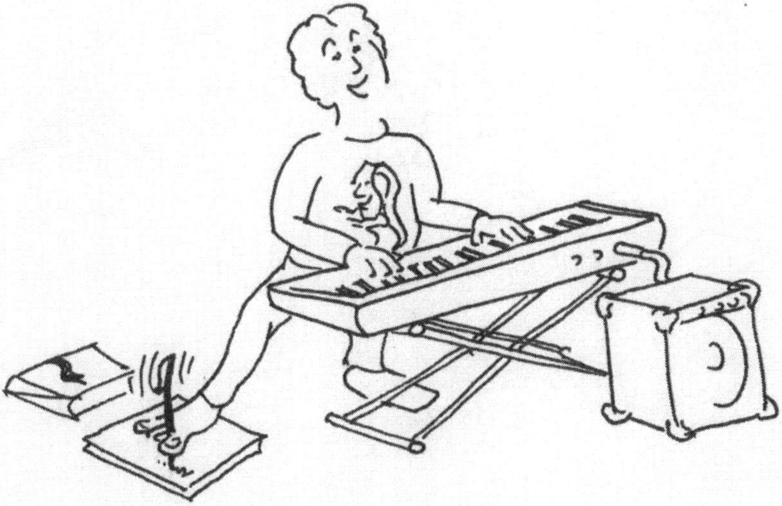

THE DREADED ADMIN

There is no getting away from the fact that although we all like to just play and sing lots of good songs a certain amount of admin is involved in running anything and a band is no exception. As I am a lawyer in my day job I am used to forms and pieces of paper generally so I probably had more paper than is really necessary but here is a list with explanations of the pieces of paper we used. Some of them we only developed towards the end as the law on working with children became more specific about some requirements. This list is here to help and not put you off. I found it soon became routine.

1. A notebook to write down who goes to each rehearsal and what you played there. I also included details of where we went to play at events and services and what we played there as well. The entries can be very short indeed but can be lengthy if you feel inspired and have the time. I still have these notes and they are very valuable for working out just where your last 70 Tuesday evenings have gone. I used them as the basis for the statistics that I put in the annual report (see 2 below) and the list of what we had played was useful to avoid too much repetition and to remind me of what had worked and what hadn't

2. The annual report. I wrote one every year to pull together what we had done and to have something to show to other people so that they could see what we had done. I do not think that this is essential at all but I do enjoy looking back over them and I have put one or two into this book at the end of the relevant chapters, so you can see how they changed over the years as we got the hang of things.

3. The band newsletter. This started off as a weekly thing which was hopelessly ambitious and strictly for the masochists out there. Believe me, running the band is hard and time consuming enough and we found that they just got made into paper aeroplanes which was a bit annoying. We settled on doing a newsletter when we had something to say whether this was because an event was coming up or because we had done an event and wanted to pass on info to the band. I tried to make them as entertaining as possible within limits but at first my computer ability was very limited. With the subsequent band that I set up (Anything in G) I did a monthly newsletter in publisher format which seemed about the right length and frequency.

Remember remember the 8th of November

Volume 1 Issue 19 *8th November 2002*

THE STATISTICS CONTINUED

SONGS PLAYED IN WORSHIP

I WILL BUILD MY CHURCH (AND YES ROS'S LOT DID SING THE LOUDEST! OH NO THEY DIDNT - OH YES THEY DID!)

PRAISE HIM ON THE TRUMPET

BE STILL

I'M SPECIAL

S I N G HALLELUJAH

LORD I LIFT YOUR NAME ON HIGH

WATCH OUT FOR THIS SHEEP AT OUR NEXT ROLLERCOASTER AND MAKE SURE WE DONT LOSE HIM (OR HER!)

Traffic jam and bonfire decimate band!!

The 8th November saw the trusty band down to just four as the traffic jams of Birmingham and the temptations of the Book Group bonfire party took their toll. This does show just how successful the Band is as otherwise the dark forces at work would have no need to put these temptations in our path. As it was we were able to benefit from Ros's rather strained attempts to sound like Nick on the violin (no she doesnt) and to look like three band members instead of one. The sketch involved a considerable suspension of disbelief as we had to imagine Gloria as an old woman! Despite her attempts to avoid the aerobics during Sing Hallelujah by claiming that she is a pensioner (and Hazel quickly trying to jump on to that particular band wagon) we all know you are only as old as you feel which must make me about 91 some days. However, good trumphed over evil (as always). Not only did the service contain some very lively worship (especially when Gloria liberated the percussion instruments for Praise Him on the Trumpet) but the Unohick practice afterwards enabled Nikki to hone her skills to perfection for the Tournament she was in the following

But its not in G wailed a Band member!!!!

CHURCH CRAWL COMING !!!!

What is it?
It is a way of having fun and raising money for charity as well as enjoying fellowship with lots of other Christians

What happens?
The Band moves round as many churches as possible on a Sunday morning playing at least one song or hymn in each service

Is it ecumenical?
Oh - very

Has it been done before?
Yes by the illustrious Elastic Band who raised over £400 for Children in Need and got on the TV as a result

So where has Baaaaaaaaat gone?

As Christmas is fast approaching the next Rollercoaster will have a pantomime feel to it (in a very Christian way of course!) You will find out just how much a hired man actually charges for looking after sheep (quite a lot is the answer) and whether it is worth going to look for lost sheep when they dont actually play any instruments. We are hoping for help from Gloria on that one. Lots of congregation participation is involved and there may be sweets involved so we look forward to seeing you there with. If you have any trusty sheep you can bring with you they may be useful!

contents

There is no right or wrong answer; you just need to know what works for you and regular e-mails or text messages might be the best thing

4. The consent forms. You will need these if you are taking the young people anywhere other than to the church premises where you normally rehearse. At first we did not have these but this was a requirement that was brought in. It never gave us a problem as we knew the parents anyway but it did give us a bit more information about any medical problems. Ideally it would be good to have a First Aid person in your leadership team but that isn't essential. We never had to deal with any injuries but perhaps we were fortunate. We also had a form for joining the band which was to give us the basic details and say a bit about how the band worked.

5. You will need to have information about who is in the band. I kept this to a minimum just so that I had contact numbers and addresses for everyone. Sue and I did think of having everyone's birthdays so that we could send them a card of some description but we never quite got round to it. We did do band Christmas cards for all the members and tried to think of something band like to say. This wasn't essential but was something we felt we wanted to do.

6. I did keep a list of all the events we played at and all the songs we played at each and that was very useful if only to look back on at the end of each year. I also kept a photographic record of everything we did. This does need parental consent if you are photographing the under 18s. We did not need that at the time but now it would be a good idea to incorporate that into your

initial "joining the band" form when you ask for basic details.

7. You will need to decide how you want to keep your music. This can be a real pain and I don't think we ever found the perfect way to do it. The ideal way would be for everyone to have a copy of all the books you will ever want to play from but that is unlikely to happen. We used quite a wide range of materials. At one point the church purchased four copies of Mission Praise for us and as I already had one that made life simpler. I then bought some more when I found them being sold off in a discount book shop but this was only part one which consisted of songs starting with the letters A to H so we played a lot of Abba Father and Be Still just because I had the right books for everyone! There is no harm in being creative if it is practical! I also encouraged the guitarists to play from words and chords which I could produce on a computer quite easily and the singers would only need the words if they were confident about the tune or couldn't read music. Again this cut down on the amount of music we needed. I also found that the transposing instruments like clarinets and cornets needed parts writing for them as the books just had the main tunes in. This was something I was able to do myself but if you can't then it is time to ask a musician in your church to help or possibly a music teacher. This is another way to let other people know what you are doing and there is always the chance that they will be interested or at least sympathetic.

WHEN THE GOING GETS TOUGH

This is the chapter to read when you can't remember why you ever decided to do anything as stupid as running a band and you just want to give up. The first thing to realise is that we felt like that lots of times. However, because we didn't give in we now have some of the most amazing memories (and photos) and living proof that we changed the lives of a serious number of young people for the better. It doesn't get any better than that.

SO here are just some of the things that went wrong and what we did to keep going.

On a practical level

- We didn't have anywhere to rehearse
- We didn't have any music books
- There weren't enough hours in the day to do all the admin
- We didn't have anyone to look after our daughter who was too young to come to the rehearsals
- We did get criticised once for leaving tinsel on the church carpet

Solutions

- Ask the parents of all the band members
- Ask your church

- Do a fund raiser to raise money for books
- Check to see if your church has a licence that will enable you to copy music
- Ask sympathetic non-musicians if they will help with admin – they may be thrilled to help and even more thrilled at not having to do the youth work side of things
- If you need a babysitter ask the older church members whose children have grown up – they may actually look forward to being with children they can hand back
- Pray and then do all the above again (this does actually work!!)
- Live with the tinsel comment

On a more fundamental level

- Some church members may be resistant to the type of music you are playing
- Some church members may find offensive the use of dance and flags during services and may say they won't attend services at which the band is playing
- Some church members may be uncomfortable with the attitudes of some of the young people if the youngsters are not regular church attenders

Solutions

- Communicate on every possible occasion with the church attenders who are struggling with the use of the band – our experience was that they wanted to encourage the youngsters but really struggled with the new ways – talking really did help

- Really listen to the criticism and ask for specifics – sometimes this will be helpful and if it isn't constructive it's ok to say so and ask for some constructive criticism

- Do your research – the Old Testament has a lot to say about numbers of musicians, dance and movement – we wrote a sketch on this subject with lots of biblical references and this helped to change attitudes – if you want to use the sketch contact us

- Work very hard on your attitudes and the attitudes of the band members – model a good attitude towards the people who are struggling

- Use some of the good old songs as well as the new stuff just make sure the songs are really good and the words are still appropriate

- Use some old songs but with a different beat – a good one for this is Stand up Stand up for Jesus although it is on the militaristic side for me

- Make sure your young people have a good grounding in Christian attitudes and practices – we did a youth alpha course with the young people who had not attended the Just Looking course

- Speak to your vicar/minister and anyone else sympathetic to explain the problems and seek support – this must be done sensitively and is not to be an exercise in divide and rule – do it on a no names basis

- Pray pray AND pray again – these are spiritual difficulties and must be addressed in the right spirit
- Look into your own heart – provided your attitudes are right then press on – sometimes it is important that new attitudes to worship are respected – one of our greatest supporters was the Bishop of Salisbury and that encouraged us when we were being criticised
- Bear in mind that the critics may be more vocal than the supporters but are also likely to be less numerous – don't over react
- Sometimes its ok to cry – I did reach that point more than once and found it helpful to cry out to God in prayer and ask for His help and comfort – you will get it

The really big stuff

- One of the band members wants to leave
- All of the band members want to leave
- You want to leave

Solutions

- It's a good idea to plan for this when you decide on your vision for the band. It is obvious that a vision that the band will last forever is unhelpful and pointless. Provided your vision is workable (as ours proved to be) then if one person leaves that does not mean that the band is a failure
- Having said that it is still concerning when people stop coming or say that they are thinking of leaving. The

first thing to say is that the Elastic Band is elastic. It is not a worship group with clearly defined (and sometimes very exclusive) boundaries. If someone has been a band member then they stay a band member even if they no longer come to practices. The consequences of this are that your attitude to them must not change in any way. They are still loved, respected and prayed for. That way the door is always open if they choose to return (and in our experience some people will). Even if they don't return the chances are that they will have positive memories of the band . Young people are fully entitled to grow change and develop in their own time. Any time they choose to share with you and the band is valuable.

- If lots of the band want to leave then you need to know why. The one time this happened to us was when our older members wanted to start their own Christian band. Sue and I were thrilled when this happened. So bear in mind that band members wanting to stop coming to rehearsals may be a brilliant thing

- If you want to stop running the band you have to think long and hard about this. With the benefit of hindsight (and isn't that a wonderful thing) it is a good idea to say at the start that you will run the band for a certain period (three years would be my preference now). At the end of that period you can choose to carry on for another fixed period but it gives you a very useful framework. Sue and I stopped when Sue and her family moved away. There was no one else who wanted to step into her shoes and so it was the only choice. If you do decide to stop the band either before the end of a fixed period or if you have no fixed period there is a lot to think about. Make sure everyone in the band and the church understands that this is happening so that there are no mixed messages. Prepare a report for the church to enable them to benefit from your experience. Have an end of band celebration of some sort. Prepare to feel very sad even if you are worn out with running the band. You will miss the young people and the worship both in services and in practices. Look forward to how your relationships with the young people will carry on. I see three of our old band members on a very regular basis and really value their friendship.

- Another alternative to stopping the band is to have a break for a set period. This will give you time to re focus and will enable people to see what it is about the band that they miss. This will then encourage them to appreciate what the band has to offer when you start again. This is not something which Sue and I ever did but we would have been willing to consider it. We deliberately did not stop the band during school holidays as we wanted to demonstrate a way of life rather than have similarities with a school schedule. However, this was tough and a scheduled break could have been a good idea.

THE MASSIVE STUFF

There is always the possibility that a band member will want to talk to you about some form of abuse that he or she is suffering. You need to think about this when you are setting up the band at the beginning. Make contact with your child protection officer, explain what you are planning to do and ask them for any advice they can give you. Discuss with them how to contact them urgently should any problems arise. It is important that you have a good relationship so that you can ask them for advice if an unusual situation arises. To avoid problems within the band make sure that you have guidelines in place about sensible systems of working. For example, make sure that you are not alone with one other band member in any situations that could be misinterpreted. Make sure your CRB checks are in place.

Despite all that we have said in this section about the problems they never exceeded the pleasure and satisfaction we got from running the band. There were many hurdles we had to overcome but they taught us faith, patience, forgiveness and resilience – not bad things to develop. They also taught us the value of prayer and that is a lesson worth learning.

PASTORAL CARE

As you will have realised the pastoral care of the young people in the Band is crucial. The ethos behind the Band is that the Band is a vehicle to introduce young people to the concept of a loving God. Unless they see that love reflected in their leaders they will not be able to understand the concept. Because we are only human we will fail at times to show that love but the leaders must strive at all times to demonstrate that love. The ways in which we did this (and we are not saying that these were the best or the only ways) were as follows

1. We accepted anyone into the band and worked out with them what they had to offer

2. We respected their views and if they differed from our own we talked the issues through with them. Examples included listening to satanic rock and discussing it with them discussing whether all traditional hymns are boring and challenging them to find interesting ways of playing them

3. We listened to their problems and concerns and tried to help them work out solutions. Examples included health issues for family members, exams and issues around the death of a young person in the village that they knew

4. We sent Christmas cards

5. We ran the Band, looked for opportunities for the Band and enabled the Band to play in different places and for different events

6. We allowed them a certain amount of lee way (and probably too much) in their behaviour. We wanted the Band to be fun and energised and therefore we did not want to be too didactic. This meant that at times there could be a lot of noise and a certain amount of chaos. We were picked up on this by the parents but found it possible to work through the problem. There is always a fine line on this one but my preference was always for the young people to want to come and both Sue and I were prepared to work hard at keeping the Band lively

7. We asked for their suggestions on what the Band should do. Some of the best things we did including the church crawl came from their suggestions

8. We asked for their help when we got stuck with something especially when we were trying to work out how to use notation programmes on computers!

9. We listened to their feedback and answers to questionnaires. If it was possible to change something we changed it.

10. We put them into situations that were demanding and prayed for and with them to enable them to have the confidence to succeed. Looking back it astonished me that from our very small beginnings we reached the point where we felt confident enough to play at Festivals and entertain in excess of 150 children and young people. They repaid our trust many times over.

11. We prayed for them a lot both when we were with them and when we were not.

RELATIONSHIPS WITH OTHERS

One of the most difficult aspects of running the Band is keeping track of all the different people you need to keep in mind. The most helpful thing I can do is to list them all. How you decide to handle those relationships is for you to decide and will depend on your own personal circumstances. This is where the words SERVANT MINISTRY need to be engraved on your heart (or perhaps tattooed on your forehead!!)

1 God

Prayer and reading the bible especially the Old Testament was what got us through

2 The leadership of your church.

This could include the vicar, church wardens, PCC, elders, Minister, curate etc etc. All of these people have an official role within the church which is to be respected. They can be invaluable to you if you test your plans and ideas with them particularly where you are treading new ground. The chances are that they will be very supportive and also able to point out any pitfalls that you had not foreseen. They will also be able to help you deal with any problems but it is far easier for them if they are forewarned if you are attempting something unusual. I got this badly wrong once when picking entirely new music for a major festival service (harvest festival). If only I had had the common sense to talk this through with a church leader I could have avoided an obvious mistake

3 Parents of Band members

It goes without saying that they are very important people in the life of the Band. Some will be church attendees themselves and some will not. Therefore you may be extending your ministry to them without even being aware of it. They are letting you spend time with their children who are very precious to them. Value them and ask for their help whenever possible. They may well help with transport, sound checks, coming up with suggestions for band activities, helping with barbecues and picnics, providing reviews of band activities. We were very fortunate with the parents of our band members. We could not have done what we did without them.

4 Church congregation

Members who are not in leadership roles and are not parents of band members - they will either love the Band, accept the Band even though they struggle with it or find it baffling and in some cases unacceptable. We did find it hard when we were told that some people really disliked the Band but simply decided that what we were doing was important and provided it was clear when the Band was or was not playing then people had to make their own decisions about whether to attend the service. In numerical terms this problem was not a major one.

5 Children and Youth workers from other areas

These were a great bunch of people to know. They were supportive and by liaising with them we came up with some excellent opportunities for the Band. Networking is very worthwhile

6 Shop assistants in music shops and people who work in recording studios

I have grouped these together as I met all of them at various times and was unfailingly surprised at how interested and sympathetic they were. Evangelism never ends and even just telling these people about what you are doing and why is spreading the gospel message. The assistant at the music shop really enjoyed hearing about what we were doing and I slowly built up a full set of shakers each of which was a different fruit or vegetable from the stock in the shop which I use to this day (the carrot and banana are particularly good shapes for shakers).

7 People who work at sports centres and in places used for after gig debriefs

The same message applies here - provided you let them know what you are doing and why you will be giving out a very positive message. When we had the praise party at the pool we made up a tape of worship songs which was played on the sound system. We received very positive feedback from the lifeguards who were very surprised at the quality of the songs.

SO HOW MUSICAL DO YOU HAVE TO BE?

The Band needs a minimum of two leaders. Of those one and preferably no more than one needs to be a competent musician. They do not need to be a music teacher and if they are it is important that they leave the day job behind. It is good if they are competent on keyboard or guitar even if that is not their main instrument as they will be able to sing or speak whilst playing. They do not need any formal musical training but need to be able to play a recognisable introduction, and work out simpler parts for the less experienced musicians in the band. It is useful if they can tune a violin or find out how to.

The Band gives a lot of opportunity to experiment musically and to write simple songs so the more adventurous will not get bored. We wrote action songs and songs where the congregation supplied some of the words during the service. However, it is completely acceptable to use existing material only. Spring Harvest, Mission Praise, Ishmael, Songs of Fellowship, Out of the Ark all produce excellent music that can be enjoyed by young people and adults as well.

It does no harm at all to work on your own level of musical skills whilst running the Band but it is not necessary to be a professional level musician to run the Band. If you have some skill and a desire to run a band my advice would be to start your band and see how far you get rather than wait until you are completely happy with your own skill level. That way you will have playing opportunities which will improve your playing and the pleasure of enjoying the Band.

THE SPIRITUAL SIDE

I realise that as religious books go this book is not full of Bible references. It is very much a "how to" guide based on experience. However, the ethos of the Band is based on a number of significant passages that underpin the work that was done. The key verses are:

Psalm 8 verses 1 to 2:

O Lord, our Lord,
Your greatness is seen in all the world!
Your praise reaches up to the heavens;
It is sung by children and babies.
You are safe and secure from all your enemies;
You stop anyone who opposes you.

Psalm 15 verses 3 to 6:

Praise Him with trumpets
Praise Him with harps and lyres
Praise Him with drums and dancing
Praise Him with harps and flutes
Praise Him with harps and cymbals.
Praise Him with loud cymbals
Praise the Lord all living creatures!
Praise the Lord!

Matthew 18 verses 2 to 3:
Mark 10 verse 15:
Luke 18 verse 17:

So Jesus called a child, made him stand in front of them and said "I assure you that unless you change and become like a child you will never enter the kingdom of heaven"

2 Samuel verse 5:

David and all the Israelites were dancing and singing with all their might to honour the Lord. They were playing harps, lyres, drums, rattles and cymbals.

I read the Bible cover to cover before I started the Band. The verses I have set out above were the ones that stayed with me. We are commanded to praise God, to use instruments, to dance and sing and to become as children. In running the Band I was attempting to do all these things. We wanted to maintain the freshness and energy of youth and to praise God without reservation. This we did both in the services and during our rehearsing. In my view this had the effect of releasing throughout our church a spiritual energy which fed into and upon other activities within the church. The Band gave other people in the congregation permission to worship in a less inhibited way and to experience new songs and new ways of using music and movement. It enabled us to visit other places, and have fellowship with other Christians of all ages. It was a very freeing experience which I still remember with gratitude and pleasure. It is my belief that if similar bands were to be set up in other places both in the UK and elsewhere this would result in a tremendous release of spiritual power. I believe that young people are not experiencing the full joy that can be theirs when they have a chance to join an Elastic Band. I do not underestimate the amount of work that is involved in running the Band because I have done it. However, I do not believe that Sue and I are (or at least were!) the only people with that level of commitment and energy. It is not for the faint hearted but it brings a level of pleasure, joy and satisfaction that is almost impossible to quantify. If you have any desire at all after reading this book to start a band I would urge you to do so and I will be willing to support you in your efforts. You will be obeying God's command and that cannot fail to bring blessings upon you.

HOW TO GET STARTED

It is quite possible that you will have lots of ideas about how to do this but just in case you haven't this is how to go about it. The Band I ran after the Elastic Band was started exactly like this.

1. Find one or more like minded people. If you are the musician they do not need to be. If you are not the musician they will need to be. Pray with them and any other like minded people and ask for God's guidance as you plan how the Band is to operate.

2. Decide how long you want to run the Band for (three years is a good starting point), when and where you want to meet and plan the activities for your first three sessions (see How to Rehearse and How Not to Rehearse)

3. Speak to the children and youth leaders in your church if any and find out who might be interested in joining the Band. Speak to each young person and see if they are interested. If there is no youth work or children work going on at all speak to the church leadership to track down children who might be interested.

4. Speak to your child protection officer and make sure the checks you need are in place and ask advice about what records to keep. Check out the church insurance policy.

5. Start meeting and start your diary.

6. Make sure that you do not have any services to play for, for at least the first six weeks so that your focus really is on the band members and not the music.

7. Have fun.

There is no doubt that your band will be different from any others but as long as it remains an elastic band it will be amazing.

THE VIEW FROM THE VICAR

Establishing any form of church youth work can be a struggle. Attempting it in a rural context can be an even greater challenge. So to be able to look back at a time when youth work was not only viable but actually one of the key strengths is both unusual and a great joy. That is what Elastic Band did. It now occupies a valued place in the annals of history. But more importantly, its impact on the lives of members and recipients will never be fully known – at least not this side of the "pearly gates"!

For an all-too-brief period in the 1990s, its light shone in the village, the Diocese and beyond. It's at the first level that I think its impact was the most profound. It was a disarmingly simple idea – a band that was sufficiently elastic to stretch to whatever its members wanted it to be – while at the same time generating energy and stretching band members themselves. It worked fantastically well in an ecumenical context, both through membership and ministry, and across several rural Anglican parishes in a team ministry and deanery. It built friendships (though to the best of my knowledge no weddings, as yet) and challenged many to reassess the place of young people, music and ministry.

Naturally, there were also some difficulties. The obvious one is those who instinctively objected to the style of music. Some were won over by the quality of musicianship or the clear sincerity of the members. Others recognised that it had a place, even though they felt it was not for them. At times it created competitiveness: just which church would win its services when 2 or even 3 services ran at exactly the same time! And the pastoral care and support of its leaders was not always as good as it might have been.

The leaders and the band members were often challenging to those in wider church leadership in the villages. And they were usually right as well! They often demonstrated a remarkable depth and maturity of spirituality and faith. I remember one of the founder members, at the time still in his early teens, sitting next to me as part of circle when Ros asked us to each pray (out loud) for the person on our left – so he ended up praying for me. I still remember him saying, "God – I have no idea how to pray for a vicar – but here goes…" And his prayer was exactly what I needed at that point.

It seems to me four things were crucial for its operational success (as distinct from its spiritual.)

1. The boldness of the vision. At its inception, youth work was already a strength, at least in Aldbourne. But all things are relative. The combined adult population of the 6 villages of the Team Ministry was not much over 3,000 so the pool from which to fish was already small. To find young people willing to commit time and effort would be difficult. And this is where the vision of elasticity really scored.

2. Timeliness. The writer of Ecclesiastes famously wrote: "There is a time for everything and a season for every activity under heaven." (Ch 3 v1). It came at an optimum time, a convergence. The people, the opportunities, the need … But equally important was the recognition that it was time-limited. Ecclesiastes of course continues: …"a time to be born and a time to die, a time to plant and a time to uproot…" (v2) When the time came for it to end – it ended! Despite the temptations to let it run beyond its course – because end points are always easier to identify with hindsight than in the present – it finished with its reputation still intact.

3. The enthusiasm and commitment of the Band members. The Band welcomed keen members who initially perhaps had little discernable musical ability; it allowed them to feel part of the Band. And then to grow both their musicianship and their faith at their own pace. Membership was demanding. But what Ros demanded was visionary because it was much more about behaviours (commitment, enthusiasm, willingness to learn, to take responsibility and to be honest).

4. The quality of the leadership. If the Band's name reflected the flexibility of membership and style, it applied equally well to the leadership. Ros and Chris Oswald and Susie May had a further handful of leaders (and occasionally found themselves in a situation where the leaders were a handful!). It's also fair to say that much of the burden fell on Ros' shoulders – and at times it was indeed a heavy burden. Needing continuity, Ros was often the visible focus. She has all the vision and skills to do it supremely well. But there was a cost. Above all, the leaders walked the talk, they behaved in the way they wanted members to behave. And the core principle of elasticity – willingness to discuss and compromise – must have had a lingering impact on members.

Finally, do I have any reservations or regrets? We were in a rural setting sufficiently affluent for members to own their own instruments and I'm not aware of any who felt excluded or unable to apply. They were well-led. They performed an immeasurably valuable ministry in the village and beyond and gave us flexibility when planning worship, both as an input to more conventional services and in being able to broaden the range of services on offer. They were an ecumenical focus that facilitated even greater co-operation in other areas. They were well-known in the county: it was a taste of success and seemed to boost confidence and faith. They were enthusiastic, they were fun; and as the Band collectively grew in confidence and competence so that was reflected in the growth of the individual members.

So actually – no! As the vicar at the time, I am deeply appreciative of all it brought and recognise how fortunate and blessed I was, especially as a rural vicar, to have them as a resource.

PETER HYSON

VIEW FROM A PARENT, CHURCH WARDEN AND MORE RECENTLY A PARISH DEVELOPMENT CONSULTANT

As a parent it was great to have a church activity running in the village which both my boys looked forward to going to . Week by week Elastic Band provided an evening out , which helped them to develop, socially, musically and spiritually. It was a disappointment that my daughter did not stick with the band but that was due more to the relationship with her brothers than with band members or leaders.

The appearance of the band in worship was an added bonus. Parents and their children rarely find services which both enjoy. The band-led services provided just that. In retrospect I wonder why I did not attend more of the services which they led in other churches. One reason is that at the time I was also the church warden of St Michaels.

As a warden the band posed a few more issues. Despite my enjoyment of the services led by the band this enjoyment was not shared by every member of the church. Then, as now, there is a range of preferences when it comes to liturgy and whereas now there is greater tolerance of other styles, then it was a different matter. Open hostility was rare but mutterings were more common. The music was too loud; the music was inappropriate; the songs were meaningless or irreverent; the happy-clappy services were too frequent and so on. Besides services there were other issues too. I was happy to unlock the church and turn the heating on (inadequate though it was) but others were heard to ask who was paying for the heating and lighting; some were concerned about young people running all over the building and some spotted graffiti on the wall inside the Church!

I hope I steered a course through this minefield. As church warden I could see the benefit of having young people experience a relevant church with generous leaders and to have access to the Christian story through the songs and discussion. The fact that for many band members this was their only contact with church was of enormous significance. On the other hand for the more traditional church members, they were the ones who supported the church financially and did many of the practical tasks involved in its upkeep. As members of the body of Christ they too needed care.

As a parish development officer for ten years now I look back at the era of the Elastic Band with immense gratitude for what the leaders did then. I also feel some sadness that, as a church, we did not do more to help it blossom and maybe adapt and grow rather than let it end. The fact that the first band formed a new band and the original band evolved could have become a model for further growth. Young people love to do things in groups and it is not uncommon for one group to grow up and remain together until they move away. The band provided a brilliant vehicle for helping the younger ones join something so the process could have been repeated over and over again with new groups.

The Elastic Band was a genuine "Fresh Expression of Church" years before such a term was coined. For the youngsters involved and its leaders this was church; they worshipped together, prayed, learned and grew in fellowship and discipleship. Had we known then what we know now about Fresh Expressions it might have been an even more remarkable story.

I regret that we did not gather a team of people who made it their business to support the project from the start. The team may or may not have involved the leaders of the band. (They needed to meet regularly anyway to maintain the flow of activity week by week). The team could have acted as a bridge between the band and the wider church. Its purpose would have been to support the leaders in a variety of ways.

- Listening to the needs of the band and seeking to find resources as needed
- Sharing the aims with the wider church and seeking support both in prayer and practical ways such as sorting music, helping set up practices, providing transport etc
- Through involvement in support roles encourage helpers to become involved in more central activities so that apprentices could become leaders.
- (The original leaders could have moved while the band lived on, when they felt fresh callings on their time)
- Seeking financial support from the PCC and permissions to be involved in events throughout the year
- Helping with the promotion of events and seeking to make more of them through provision of add-ons such as refreshments, bookstalls, recording etc

The latest fresh expression in our village is Messy Church and I hope the leaders will read this book, take encouragement and learn some lessons from the Elastic Band experience.

GEORGE RENDELL

VIEW FROM A YOUTH LEADER 1981 – 1997

How do you keep Christian teenagers in Church? And by this I mean "in fellowship together" and not literally in a "Church building".

At the time that Ros, Chris and Suzie were forming the "Elastic Band" we already had a good **GBH** teenage group (self-styled name standing for **G**od's **B**unch of **H**elpers) which met during the Sunday morning service and joined the congregation in church for Communion. This had worked for some time but meeting in the primary school which they had all attended was not ideal to say the least (oh, those little chairs!) and the fact that we kept them through secondary school age was entirely through the grace of God and the support of the church going parents. It was "fertile ground" time, the age of self-awareness and development of character in those difficult years, we tried to think of all the ways we could keep them involved in church.

Therefore, when the Elastic Band came along, it provided a much needed break from anything that in any way resembled "Sunday School". With a different format and forum its members flourished into a vibrant youth group. The GBH group continued and even grew for a while as these young people not only explored and developed their talents but also their spirituality. Elastic Band was something they did independently rather than with their parents. It as just what we needed for that all important "next stage".

We'd done some drama with GBH which Ros further developed and that, along with their musical talents, not only produced multi-talented young people but also provided the churches with an amazing resource which eventually led to major musical/drama productions, Christian and non-Christian.

I enjoyed witnessing their "Church" being in fellowship together especially at events such as those held in Salisbury Cathedral, where they met many other young people who they could relate to and be free to worship together without censorship from their peers. This is such a blessing and I believe there is nothing more valuable today than young people feeling they can express their faith in a way that is acceptable to their generation.

Breaking out of Sunday School is always a difficult moment. Most teenagers never return to mainstream church and some only return in later life. To keep young people in worship is difficult and an age old problem. Our set Anglican services do not generally appeal and we are always having to invent new ways to keep, or bring back in, those who have wandered off. Elastic Band did just that, it kept them in communion with God and each other, providing a valuable role for each of those members within the life of the church and the community.

Elastic Band, I think, took those young people onto the next stage of a personal relationship with God, with Jesus. A personal faith, that in their formative years must have set them up for life or, at the very least, started them on their own personal journey.

MARGARET HILL

SO HOW WAS IT FOR YOU?

We asked the Band members in 2013 to let us know what being in the Band meant for them. Here are the questions and replies

Question One

As a result of being in the Band did you
(a)Attend more church services than you otherwise would

Question One replies:
(a)

- Yes I especially enjoyed going to other churches outside Aldbourne
- Although it may not have resulted in me attending more church services I think it helped get to know other people who were attending the services and enjoy them more as a result.
- Yes
- To be totally honest my parents were the ones who decided how many services we attended but I am sure I was more willing to attend as I enjoyed being part of the band
- Although it may not have resulted in my attending more church services, it helped me to enjoy them more
- Yes

- **Yes**

(b) Find out things about yourself you didn't know before (all answers accepted including that you couldn't play an F#minor chord quickly)

- **The mic will still pick you up when you are talking instead of playing**
- **It made me confident that I was able to play in front of a crowd (even if hiding behind a drum kit)**
- **Realised I was any good**
- **I think Elastic Band confirmed my love of music. I had piano lessons from a young age and always liked music but having the opportunity to play with others made it even more special.**
- **The mic will still pick you up when you are talking, not playing (yes, it's duplicated!) and**
- **I like sitting down and if you play guitar, you have to stand up.**
- **Sign language and to some extent dealing with never before performing (though I also did this with other hobbies)**

Question 2

What was it about playing for others (in Aldbourne and elsewhere) that you enjoyed

Question 2 replies

- Its hard to pinpoint specific things but I do remember really enjoying joining in with others and feeling like other people enjoyed listening to our music.
- It was really good to play with the band and get to know other people in the band.
- It built my confidence.
- It was great for me to build confidence and a lot of fun
- running round the church with ribbons is great fun.
- I found out for the first time that I really enjoy working on a song and learning it properly which we did when we got the rock score for Bryan Adams' "Everything I Do". I also really enjoyed playing on the back of a Church Float at the carnival. We were jilted about a lot and it was really good fun.
- Doing it with my friends.

Question 3

Did you learn Christian songs you didn't know before

Question 3 replies

- I hadn't had the opportunity to play or hear contemporary Christian songs live before Elastic Band.
- Not sure
- Yes

- **Yes**
- **Yes**
- **Yes**

Question 4

If you were to have or already have children (and how old does that make us feel!) would you want them to have the chance to be in an Elastic Band

Question 4 replies

- **I would very much like them to have the opportunity to join such a friendly fun atmosphere and learn about the church and the Bible in a fun way -I am 4.5 months pregnant so thinking about children a lot these days! I would love to find something like Elastic Band that my children could be involved in.**
- **Yes.**
- **Yes of course it was a great way to learn about faith, music, to make friends and stay busy and out of trouble (hopefully!)**
- **Yes**
- **Yes**
- **Yes**

Question 5

Did being in the Band help you to learn more about the church

Question 5 replies

- Yes. It made me realise that it could be fun.
- Yes most importantly that it is fun.
- Yes in particular Aldbourne church.
- Yes I don't like tinsel
- Yes, it helped me to learn how the church should be
- Yes, like the other person it helped me to learn how the church should be.
- Yes

Question 6

Did being in the Band help you to learn more about Christianity

Question 6 replies

- Yes. It made me realise that there are many different ways to express faith.
- Yes
- Yes
- Yes, I think it did, especially about the importance of community
- Because I have studied Christianity since being in the Band (eg attending an Education for Ministry course) after all this time it is difficult to tell how much I learned in the Band and how much I learned later.
- Yes

Question 7

Did being in the Band help you to learn more about the importance of faith

Question 7 replies

- **Definitely and this stays with me today**
- **Yes**
- **Yes**
- **Yes, I think it did. It can bring happiness and joy.**
- **Yes**
- **Yes**

Generally:

I thoroughly enjoyed it!
I think for a small village it was a perfect way to introduce musicians of different ages into playing as a group. It also gave me many opportunities to see live music from a young age.
I am still in touch with other Band members

EPILOGUE

I have tried to set out, warts and all, the challenges you may encounter but these are by far outweighed by the rewards for the young people you work with, for your church and for you personally.

My memories of the Elastic Band are precious to me, but in the course of writing this book and talking to ex members who are now adults and parents themselves, and also to others in the village, I came to the realisation that the benefits for them and our community generally were more significant and longer lasting than I had ever realised.

If you want to do something but don't know how - ask people. You will be amazed how helpful people want to be. Doors will open in directions you don't expect - don't be afraid to have a peep through - if God wants it to happen, He will find ways of making it work through you.

The Elastic Band fulfilled many ambitions for me but left me with only one: to hear from as many people as possible who are enjoying their own Elastic Band Journeys.

The unfamiliar can be scary and I am saddened at the thought that many people may have had the same ideas as me but never started, so if there is any message I can leave you with, it would be this:

Just Do It, and Enjoy the Ride!